Give A Horse A Second Chance

Adopting and Caring For Rescue Horses

J. R. Wise

THE LYONS PRESS
Guilford, Connecticut
An imprint of The Globe Pequot Press

Copyright © 2007 by J. R. Wise

The Lyons Press is an imprint of The Globe Pequot Press

10 9 8 7 6 5 4 3 2 1

Printed in the United States of America

Designed by [if applicable]
ISBN-13: 978-1-59228-977-6
ISBN-10: 1-59228-977-0

Library of Congress Cataloging-in-Publication Data is available on file.

Contents

Introduction

I wrote this book for anyone who has ever rescued a horse with health and safety issues. However, most of the information is intended for the experienced horse owner. I hope that first-time horse owners will find this book useful, but the job of rescuing severely neglected and abused horses should be undertaken by people with horse-care experience and training expertise. Caring for a severely neglected horse can be dangerous, expensive, and time consuming. Family support, disposable income, sturdy facilities, and enough land to keep the animal healthy and happy are essential. First-time owners might consider volunteering at a horse rescue facility to gain experience before taking on such a large responsibility. Riding lessons and training clinics will also help provide horse-care and handling knowledge. Information can be gained from training tapes and books, but finding a skilled mentor is an essential part of learning good horsemanship.

This book covers the adoption, care, and training of rescue horses. I have had over thirty years of experience caring for horses, including a few rescue horses, but this book would not have been possible without the assistance of equine practitioner Dr. Michael Frederick, and natural horsemanship trainer and clinician, Dan Bowman. Their expertise and advice have been invaluable.

Adopting Horses from Rescue Organizations

A Second Chance for Missy

Jenny Doe is still trying to recover from the financial effects of a nasty divorce, and now it looks as though her job will soon be outsourced to a third-world country. Worse news: the owner of the boarding stable where Jenny keeps her horse is doubling the rent. Jenny could barely afford the original amount and simply can't afford to keep her beloved mare Missy anymore. The realization is painful but inescapable.

Jenny's children will be heartbroken. Missy has always been the perfect companion animal and a gentle, patient babysitter. She loves children and always stands quietly while the little ones crawl all over her. Missy is perfectly content to carry them around in slow, careful circles in exchange for a couple of carrots and a bit of attention.

Missy deserves a good home, and Jenny is determined to find one with responsible people who will appreciate the gentle little mare. Missy has never met an unkind person and thinks all human beings are just wonderful. Jenny can't bear the thought of betraying that trusting heart and selling her to the first yahoo to come along in search of a "hairy motorcycle."

In the Doe family living room stands an old display case crowded with fading trophies and happy memories. Jenny and Missy won the trophies at local horse shows many years ago. Finding a home for Missy wouldn't have been a problem back then, when she was still a valuable show horse. But Missy is now twenty-two years old.

If she had a choice, Jenny wouldn't take a million dollars for Missy, let alone the few hundred dollars the elderly mare might bring at a horse sale. Instead of settling for a bargain-basement price, she contacts an equine rescue facility in her area and gets some good news. Not only will the facility be happy to take Missy, but they will also screen the gentle little mare for a special riding therapy program.

Equine therapy programs for special-needs children have been springing up all around the country. Children with debilitating diseases often benefit immensely from equine therapy because horseback riding exercises many of the same muscles that are used in walking. In other programs, at-risk children learn patience, responsibility, and self-control by working with horses. Riding therapy is also lots of fun. Gentle, steady horses are required for this work. If all goes well, and Missy passes the therapy facility screening process, she will spend the rest of her days doing what she loves best, surrounded by children.

Kelsey Jones was trapped in a dysfunctional, violent family and lived in constant pain and fear until a highly dedicated social worker rescued her at the age of eight. With the support and encouragement of child welfare staff, Kelsey managed to help save her own life by stammering out a laundry list of horrors to the custody hearing judge, but she has barely spoken to anyone else since that terrifying day in court.

One of the counselors involved with Kelsey's therapy has observed that the little girl often draws pictures of horses. Kelsey spends much of the day with her crayons, drawing endless pictures of the same little white mare.

Kelsey's counselor wonders if the child might benefit from an equine therapy program. Emotionally disturbed children will often respond to animals when human beings seem much too threatening. The counselor knows that horses have started the healing process in the shattered hearts of many abused children. Children on horseback experience a feeling of freedom previously unknown in their lives. Carefully supervised riding therapy also helps build confidence, coordination, and self-control.

The counselor who takes Kelsey to visit the therapy center is happy to discover that the facility has recently taken delivery of a white mare whose appearance somewhat resembles the little girl's artwork.

Actually, Missy is a light gray color, though almost white from age. Kelsey gives a squeal of delight when she is introduced to the mare, and Missy lowers her head to gently nuzzle the child's hair and cheek with her soft nose. The mare stands quietly while Kelsey pets and brushes her soft coat. She is perfectly content to carry the little girl around in slow, careful circles, in exchange for a bit of attention and a couple of carrots.

After a few months of equine therapy, Kelsey is gaining confidence, and the exercise is improving her health. The little girl is finally starting to come out of her shell. Equine therapy has helped to set her free. She can carry on short conversations, and she is becoming passionately articulate on the subject of horses.

The preceding fictional story is based on just one of many common scenarios in which responsible horse owners need to find good homes for their animals and decide to entrust care of their animals to equine rescue facilities.

Homeless family pets, retired show horses, ex-racehorses, and even mustangs—all kinds of horses can be found at equine rescue and adoption facilities. Though some may have been seized from neglectful caretakers, others are donated by responsible owners who want a safe haven for their beloved horses. Owners donate their horses to such facilities knowing that they will receive quality care until they can be adopted by responsible families.

The personnel staffing equine rescue facilities put quite a bit of effort into finding good homes for the horses in their care. Most rescue organizations carefully screen potential adopters, inspect the adopters' facilities, and continue to monitor the care the horse receives after it is placed into a new home. Many rescue horses make good companion animals for the average horse person, and they can be acquired at a modest initial cost.

Why Adopt a Horse?

Rescue horses deserve a second chance, and horse lovers have the satisfaction of knowing they can save a horse's life by providing a good home. There is also a wide selection of horses to choose from. Just about every breed of equine is available for adoption at various rescue facilities, from tiny Shetland ponies to massive Belgian draft horses.

Many equine athletes are ready and waiting to begin second careers. Retired thoroughbred race horses have been successfully retrained as show horses. Standardbred harness-racing horses have been retrained and shown successfully in every discipline from dressage to team penning. Retired show horses often have second careers as family horses, and they make excellent companions for novice adults and children.

Rescue horses including registered horses, such as thoroughbreds, standardbreds, and quarter horses, can usually be obtained for a reasonable adoption fee. Most adoption fees are under $1,000. Fees vary according to how much effort and expense is involved in preparing a horse for adoption. Untrained mustangs, for example, may be obtained for the basic Bureau of Land Management (BLM) fee of $125. However, gentled mustangs, including saddle horses, are available at certain BLM adoption sites for higher fees. (See page 18 for more on mustang rescues.) Transport costs may also be included in the fee. For example, pregnant mares' urine (PMU) rescue facilities transport foals and mares from PMU ranches across the Canadian border to holding facilities in the United States. They may purchase the animals from auctions, or directly from PMU ranches. Basic needs such as food, shelter, and vet care must also be met, and charitable donations do not always cover these expenses. (See page 15 for more on PMU rescues.)

Another advantage to adopting a horse from a rescue facility is that the horse can usually be returned to the facility if the relationship doesn't work out. Depending on the specific rules of each rescue facility, all or part of adoption fees may be refunded. Rescue organizations often refund adoption fees if the adopter returns the horse within thirty days, or similar time limit, or the fee may be applied to a different horse. Adopters should make inquiries regarding return policies before adopting a horse. Some facilities may not have enough space or foster families available to support a return policy.

Locating a Legitimate Equine Adoption Facility

According to Susan Wellman, director of the American Standardbred Adoption Program, "A potential adopter should ask how long the adoption program has been in existence. Ask if they are a 501(c)(3) organization. If they are, it indicates that they have gone the extra step towards being a credible program."

The Internal Revenue Service requires 501(c)(3) organizations to be operated for charitable purposes, such as the prevention of cruelty to children or animals. Once these organizations have satisfied government requirements for eligibility, they can obtain exemption from federal income tax under section 501(c)(3) of the Internal Revenue Code.

Susan adds that "programs with years of experience should be preferred over programs that have recently sprouted up. Ask if they are affiliated with any organization that might endorse them, such as the Hooved Animal Humane Society, United States Trotting Association, Thoroughbred Retirement Foundation, or similar organizations." It is also a good idea to contact people who have adopted horses from that particular facility, and ask questions about their adoption experiences.

Research the facility's horses and policies

A potential adopter should research the selection of horses the facility has available. Ask about the breeds, ages, and sexes of available horses and the breeding policies regarding mares and stallions. Many facilities have rules against the future breeding of adopted mares and require stallions to be gelded.

Review the requirements for adoption and ask to see a copy of the adoption application. Rescue facilities are very concerned with finding lifelong, secure homes for their horses, and require the adopter to have horse-care experience. Rescue facilities may also prefer that adopters own their own land and facilities with plenty of pasture room for horses. Housing a horse at a local boarding facility may not be acceptable. Rescue organizations also have specific requirements regarding acceptable housing for horses, including the way barns and fences are constructed.

Consider whether the facility does any preparatory training on their horses. Some rescue facilities use foster families to socialize and prepare horses for adoption: others offer training on-site. Find out the specifics, such as whether horses are halter- and saddle-trained in preparation for adoption. Though some rescue organizations provide preparatory training, not all of them have access to professional trainers. A potential adopter needs to be realistic about the challenges that may come with handling an adopted horse. Love just is not enough. In addition to knowledge of basic horse care, adopters must have the time, family support, and necessary skills to deal with possible health and training issues, or have ready access to expert help. Inquire in advance regarding the rescue facility's return policy in case the adoption does not work out.

Research the facility's health guarantees

Legitimate rescue organizations will inform a potential adopter of any health problems a horse may have. Many facilities require an adopter to have a horse examined by a veterinarian before adoption at the adopter's expense. A veterinary examination before the adoption is finalized helps ensure that the adopter brings home a healthy horse capable of providing many years of recreation and companionship.

Ideally, legitimate rescue facilities adopt out their horses under controlled conditions, not on impulse, evaluate the horses using trained professionals, and notify the adopter of any preexisting health and safety problems long before the adoption is finalized. However, in some cases emergency rescue situations can make a thorough physical examination impossible. Humane considerations have top priority. A short discussion of health and safety indicators is included here for the reader's information. A more extensive list of health indicators is included in chapter two, "Caring for Rescue Horses," and a more lengthy discussion of disposition and training is included in chapter four.

The healthy, happy horse is interested in his surroundings and displays friendly curiosity towards visitors. The ears are forward, the eyes bright and soft, the neck muscles relaxed, and the legs and body quiet. Beware the stony-eyed horse that greets visitors with ears flattened, or the horse that paws and shoves at the stall door with neck snaked out to tear his visitor's shirt off. The horse with his hindquarters turned toward the stall door and his head in the farthest corner, may be antisocial or just not feeling well. Either way, the potential adopter should exercise caution. These behaviors indicate health or safety problems, and the adopter should make some pointed inquiries regarding the horse's normal behavior, health, and previous treatment. While observing the horse in his stall, be especially alert for signs of overt aggression or extreme fearfulness, either of which may indicate a history of abuse.

Check the horse's stall door for signs of damage. If the door looks like it was attacked by a giant termite, the horse may be a cribber or chronic wood chewer. Cribbers grab hold of a stall door, fence, or other surface, teeth clamped like a pit bull with a chew toy, while making loud rasping noises as they inhale. Cribbing is a destructive, chronic behavior problem that has a negative impact on the horse's health.

If possible, visit the horse at feeding time. A horse that dribbles feed or drools excessively while eating grain may have dental problems that require treatment. The teeth should be examined by an equine dentist, qualified adopter, or vet for such problems as sharp points on the molars, overbite, underbite, injuries, or infection. The dental markings on the lower incisors of a young horse will be a dark in color. An older horse's incisor cups will be pale tannish color or worn smooth. An older horse's teeth are more slanted in appearance than a younger horse's teeth.

The horse should be in good flesh, with the ribs well-covered. If all the horse's ribs can be counted and the outline of the spine and hip bones are visible, he is malnourished. This may be due to inadequate diet, dental problems, advanced age, or chronic illness. If the horse is thin due to chronic illness, the adopter might spend thousands of dollars on veterinary bills and still end up with sick horse.

A horse that shows no interest in visitors and hangs his head listlessly, sides heaving, eyes glazed with illness, has obvious health problems. Respiration should be quiet and slow, and the nostrils should be clean and dry. A runny nose, especially if the discharge is milky, is an indicator of poor health. Labored breathing is an indicator of pain or respiratory illness. The eyes should be clear and bright. Older horses may have a slight blue cast to their eyes, but a white or gray mass in an otherwise dark-colored eye could be evidence of serious health issues. A noticeable film across the eye, excessive tearing, colored discharge, squinting, swelling, and redness are also signs of eye injury or disease.

The coat should be shiny, soft, and smooth, with no bumps, irregularities, or bald patches. Bald patches, redness, skin sensitivity, bumps, crusty growths, and irregular hair growth may be signs of skin diseases. Long hair in summer may be an indicator of Cushing's disease or age-related systemic problems. Scars are evidence of previous injuries. The adopter should make inquiries regarding the history of all such injuries.

The back should be slightly concave, but not sunken or swayed in appearance. The neck should blend gracefully and smoothly into well-defined withers and muscular, sloping, shoulders. When facing the horse head on, the shoulder muscles should be equally well developed. Be suspicious of any obvious lumps or sunken-in places on the shoulder muscles, which may be evidence of past injury. The legs should have clean lines, and the tendons and muscles should be well-defined with no obvious lumps, bumps, or swelling. Warmth and swelling in the legs are indicators of ongoing problems. Definite soundness problems are indicated by limping, dragging the back feet, or head nodding. Unhealed wounds or scars in the joint areas should be regarded with deep suspicion.

More clues to soundness problems include muscle wasting on one area of a horses's body, while the opposing side is well-developed, or a peculiar stance when the horse is standing at rest. The horse may show a tendency to favor one foot, or he may try to shift his weight off a sore foot by standing with the front feet spread to either side, by holding one foot in front of the other, or by shifting his weight to the rear legs. The horse should stand square on all four feet at the end of a lead rope and be willing to move out when asked. Reluctance to move out from a standing position is likely to be an indication of behavior problems, but it might also be due to soundness problems.

The surface of the hooves should be fairly smooth, and the bottoms of the hooves should meet the ground squarely and evenly. When viewed from the side, the front surface of the hooves should be slightly convex. Seriously malformed hooves are an indicator of serious hoof disease. If the toes curl up in front and the hoof rings are unusually prominent and wide towards the heel area, and narrowing drastically towards the toes, the heel may be growing faster than the front of the hoof; this is an indication the horse may have foundered. Shallow cracks in the surface of the foot may be corrected by a farrier's attention. However, deep cracks, especially in the coronet area, are cause for great concern, as they may cause permanent interference with hoof growth.

The sole of the foot should appear slightly concave, with no obvious bulges, reddish stains, or separation between the sole material and the hoof wall. The frog of the foot should be a well-defined, hard, rubbery structure. Ragged frogs, bad-smelling pus, bulges, and hoof separations are all signs of hoof disease.

The advice of professionals—farriers, horse trainers, and veterinarians—should always be sought regarding equine health and safety issues. Rehabilitating a problem horse can be a difficult, dangerous, and expensive process. The potential adopter should seriously consider the consequences before taking on such a large responsibility, even when health and training problems appear solvable.

A list of horse rescue organizations is included at the end of this book. Many of these organizations have horses available for adoption.

The Adoption Process

The adoption process starts with an application. Most applications require that the adopter be of legal age to sign a contract. A background check may be necessary to determine a potential adopter's qualifications. Rescue organizations will not accept applicants who have been charged, let alone convicted, of animal abuse.

The adopter's experience with horses will be questioned, as well as the adopter's financial and physical ability to care for the horse. Certain standards of care are generally required. Vaccinations, worming, and farrier schedules will be reviewed. Most facilities want references, and they may contact the adopter's vet and farrier in order to obtain information about the quality of horse care provided.

Prior to approval, rescue personnel may want to come and inspect the adopter's horse facilities. The inspector will be looking for safe, sturdy fencing, adequate shelter from the elements, and enough room for exercise. Horses have a talent for injuring themselves, so pastures will be inspected for debris, such as trash, old farm equipment, or tree limbs. Sources and quality of grain, feed, and water may also be reviewed. The applicant will be asked to accept liability for any damages or injury the equine might cause, even if the rescue facility retains ownership of the animal.

Equine rescue facilities must charge adoption fees to help defray the high cost of feed, veterinary bills, housing, and equipment.

Most facilities also spend a good deal of time preparing horses for adoption.

For example, ex-racehorses, such as thoroughbreds, require a let-down period. During the let-down period, the horse's feed is changed from a high-energy to low-energy formula. Otherwise, the animal might be somewhat overstimulated for pleasure riding activities. Since most horse owners have no need to travel at 40 miles per hour across the back pasture, their horses do not require the equine equivalent of rocket fuel.

Ex-racers also need to be socialized to a herd situation with other horses, since many have been isolated in a stall for most of their lives. Stall-raised horses need time to adapt to different types of fencing barriers, such as electric wire or tape. Mustangs or other horses that have not been handled regularly need to be socialized to accept human contact.

Adopted horses often require some retraining before they can become pleasure horses. Thoroughbred racehorses are trained to push their weight into the bit as they run, so they must be taught to give to bit pressure before they can become satisfactory pleasure horses. Standardbred harness horses need to be trained to accept a saddle and rider. Some adoption facilities have on-site trainers that provide preparatory training. Other adoption facilities offer training clinics to help new owners.

Some of the horses available for adoption have had little or no training before arriving at the adoption facility. Many of the foals rescued from PMU farms have been seldom, if ever, handled. Mustangs are completely untamed, but some of the Bureau of Land Management adoption sites are now offering trained mustangs for adoption, or adopters can bring their mustangs to these facilities for training.

Rescue facility personnel will generally make every effort to match an adopter with a horse that is appropriate to the new owner's skill level. But some horses just can't get along with certain people. For example, a nervous owner and a high-strung horse are not the best combination. A flighty horse will sense his owner's anxiety and become even more neurotic.

If the adopter is a first-time owner, it is wise to bring along an experienced acquaintance to help evaluate the horse's disposition. It is also a good idea to check on the facility's return policy. Many rescue facilities will offer to exchange the horse or refund the adoption fee if the horse is returned within a certain length of time.

A veterinarian should check the animal over before the adoption is finalized. You will pay for the veterinary examination yourself, but the expense is negligible when compared with the cost of treating an unsuspected illness or chronic soundness problem.

Once everything is approved, all the papers are signed, and the adoption is finalized, you will get to take your new horse home. However, the rescue facility may still wish to stay in contact with you in order to conduct inspections or maintain oversight of the horse's welfare by other means. Some rescue organizations maintain this oversight by retaining ownership as a means of ensuring the horse is not sold or moved to inadequate facilities. Other rules may also apply. An adopter may be required to get approval from the rescue organization before moving an adopted horse, or they may not be allowed to transport a horse to a home that is too distant for regular inspections. Some organizations do not allow an adopter to breed the horse or may even limit riding activities, especially if the animal has health concerns.

Most rescue organizations expect the adopter to provide a home for life. They will not allow the adopter to sell the horse, and if the adopter is no longer able to care for the horse, the animal must be returned to the organization.

Choosing a Horse

Once the decision to adopt a horse is made, there are many types of organizations to choose from. Some rescue organizations only accept horses that have been seized by local welfare agencies. Others try to help concerned owners find new homes for their beloved animals and will accept donated horses. Many of these organizations specialize in finding homes for a particular breed of horse. Among this group are organizations that find homes for retired racehorses.

Thoroughbreds

Most racehorse owners cannot justify keeping horses that are no longer competitive. Training facilities can charge thousands of dollars per month to house these animals, and the costs can add up quickly. Not all racehorse owners own adequate facilities to retire a racehorse at home. Instead of taking these horses to the nearest sale, responsible racehorse owners may choose to donate their animals to thoroughbred retirement organizations. Such organizations prepare ex-racehorses for adoption and new careers as pleasure horses.

Thoroughbreds are highly athletic, although some bloodlines may tend to be high-strung. Thoroughbreds also are highly sensitive and responsive to patient, humane training methods. Their high degree of responsiveness, combined with suppleness and sensitivity, are qualities that help produce excellent dressage horses. Thoroughbreds' athleticism also suits them for more intense activities, such as show jumping and eventing.

Most ex-racehorses are quite used to being handled and bathed and having their feet attended to regularly. They have also been exposed to many different environments at an early age and are generally accustomed to traveling in a trailer.

Some retraining will be necessary to prepare a retired thoroughbred racehorse for a new life as a show horse or pleasure riding horse, and some rescue organizations do preparatory training before adopting a horse out. Though legitimate rescue facilities will inform you of any health problems a horse may have, soundness issues may arise due to the fact that the joints and tendons of racehorses are subjected to considerable stress over the course of a racing career.

Standardbreds

Thoroughbreds are not the only type of racehorse available for adoption. Standardbred horses, once retired from harness racing, can become wonderful riding horses. Standardbreds have good minds and are physically strong. They are well built for the trail, with good width through the loin and a reputation for endurance. At one time, they were even used as cavalry remount horses.

As a breed, standardbreds tend to be sensible horses. I have often observed standardbreds sedately pulling Amish family buggies down the road. One such horse in particular impressed me by continuing to walk calmly along while the driver of a bright red sportscar was blowing his horn and crowding the buggy. The car passed the buggy so closely that it forced the horse to stop in his tracks. Exhibiting admirable calmness under extreme provocation, the horse never turned a hair and resumed towing his family of plain folk, including small children, quietly and safely to their destination.

Susan Wellman, in addition to her duties as director of the American Standardbred Adoption Program, operates a licensed foster care home for children with emotional, physical, and mental challenges. She uses horses for therapy work, and she has found that standardbreds "seem to have a sixth sense with children."

According to Susan, racing standardbreds may start out as harness horses, but it is a mistake to pigeonhole the breed. "Only 10 percent of adopted standardbreds are used primarily as driving horses. Most families or individuals wishing to adopt a standardbred plan to use their horse for Western pleasure and trails. In the past twenty years we have seen standardbreds used as trail horses, endurance horses, show horses, drill-team horses, gymkhana mounts, roadster horses, and dressage horses."

Of course, as with any other breed, an individual standardbred's suitability as a companion animal may vary and is dependent on the animal's health, basic disposition, and prior training. A standardbred off the track will require some training to accept the weight of a rider and to learn how to correctly respond to leg cues. Most standardbred racehorses are pacers while on the track, but they are capable of traveling at a walk, trot, or canter, just like any other horse.

More information on standardbred adoption organizations, including the American Standardbred Adoption Program, is available in the appendix at the end of this book.

PMU Horses

As of this writing, certain estrogen replacement medications for women are currently being manufactured from pregnant mares' urine (PMU), though synthetic substitutes have been made available. Harvesting the raw material is labor intensive, as well as controversial. Animal welfare groups have voiced concerns that PMU mares receive inadequate exercise and are confined in narrow tie stalls for days on end, where they are unable to move around or lie down to rest. Negative publicity concerning the urine harvesting process, combined with the reported side effects of these drugs, may be factors in reduced demand for such drugs.

As individual PMU ranches are phased out, the mares used to produce the medications are in danger of being sent to slaughter. In addition, the harvesting process requires the mares to be pregnant, and the resultant foal crop is often regarded as an unwanted byproduct of the industry. Though a number of PMU ranchers are engaged in efforts to upgrade and improve their stock in order to appeal to recreational and show buyers, thousands of horses are still in jeopardy.

Many organizations are involved with the effort to rescue PMU horses and place them in loving homes. One such organization is the Equine Angels Rescue Sanctuary (EARS). EARS buys foals directly from PMU farms. The facility pays these farms extra to keep the foals with their mothers for an additional period of time. This is critical to the foals' health because they have to be transported all the way from Canada, where most of the farms are located. Frank Weller, founder of EARS, explains, "We try to have the mares and foals stay together longer, so that they come to us in better shape psychologically and physically. The foals have a long ride to our facility, though they are rested along the way."

Frank Weller is devoted to the cause of rescuing PMU mares and foals. He first became involved with PMU horses while filming a documentary on a horse rescuer. The woman was attempting to feed and care for 160 foals all by herself. She had no volunteers to help her, so Weller put down his camera, pitched in, and never looked back. Weller became a regular volunteer for the woman's organization, helping out with fundraising efforts and placing horses. He eventually went on to found EARS. The EARS facility began buying PMU foals at low-end livestock sales where the young animals were in danger of being sold for slaughter. Currently, foals are purchased directly from the farms to ensure their health and safety.

Over the years, the breeding of foals available for adoption from the EARS organization has changed. At first, most of the foals were draft crosses; nowadays more quarter horse foals are available. Many of these foals are registered and will grow up to be big, strong, beautiful Canadian Quarter Horses. Paints are also available, as are draft-cross foals produced by breeding Belgian, Clydesdale, or Percheron mares with thoroughbred or quarter horse stallions.

The foals receive all required tests and inoculations before they cross the Canadian border. After being inspected by Canadian officials, the fouls journey to the EARS facility. Once they reach the facility, the foals are rested and hydrated. Then, arrangements are made to place them in temporary foster homes.

Dedicated foster families help prepare the foals for adoption by socializing them to humans. Frank Weller describes the process: "We try to get them into foster homes as soon as possible so that they can experience a one-on-one relationship with a loving family. This is necessary because they have not received much handling at PMU farms."

A potential adopter must meet certain requirements before adopting foals from the EARS facility. Though the adopter's farm may be set up well for full-grown horses, foals have special needs. Foals are playful, curious little creatures, and have a tendency to end up in places where they don't belong. They will chew on and paw at structures in their environment. Fencing has to be foal-safe. Weller recommends diamond-weave fencing with openings too small for little hooves to fit through. Modular panels or round-pen panels will also work.

Adult PMU mares also require additional socialization and training. At the ranches, most contact with humans consists of being led into and out of the collections barns. The mares generally receive hoof care while confined in a chute and are not saddle-trained. According to Weller, "mares are also harder to socialize because they are older."

The EARS organization is in the process of developing some videotapes to help PMU adopters with training. The tapes will feature natural horsemanship-training techniques. Of course, as with any other horse, the assistance of a professional trainer should be sought whenever the safety of horse or handler may be in jeopardy.

Plans for the future of the EARS facility include funneling more PMU horses into therapy programs. Having witnessed firsthand the benefits of working with horses, Weller often says that "horses rescue us." It is his belief that horses have a "spiritual essence" and "sensitivity" that make them valuable in therapy. Autistic children who have difficulty with verbal communication often respond well to equine therapy because horses communicate by using body language. Weller also thinks that raising a PMU foal is a good family project, and working with horses helps bring families closer. More information on the EARS organization is located in the list of rescue organizations in the appendix at the end of this book.

Mustangs

The Bureau of Land Management manages wild horses on federal lands. As a part of their program, the bureau periodically rounds up and distributes mustangs to various holding areas around the country where they can be adopted by private citizens.

Sure-footed and tough, mustangs tend to be easy keepers with few health problems. With the right training, they make excellent riding horses. They are also extremely intelligent horses. Be advised that mustangs have been known to outsmart human beings on any number of occasions. For that reason, it is necessary to have some training experience before taking on a mustang. Fortunately, most mustangs are quite trainable because of the way they grow up in herd society.

Living in the wild has taught these horses that survival depends on paying close attention to the behavior of the lead horses in the herd. Dominant horses communicate with other horses by using body language, directing and driving them toward food and water and away from danger. Mustangs have to find their place in a cooperative herd society in order to survive, a lesson that carries over into training.

Adopting Gentled Mustangs

Gaining a wild horse's trust and cooperation takes time and patience. Those who intend to take on the challenge of gentling wild horses would be well advised to attend a horse-training clinic, at the very least, before adopting a mustang. Even experienced horse people may not feel mentally, physically, or emotionally equal to the task of gentling a wild horse, and they might prefer to seek the assistance of a professional horse trainer.

For those adopters who would like to have some expert help with wild horse training, gentled mustangs are available at certain adoption sites. The Bureau of Land Management has authorized a special group of people to train wild horses in preparation for adoption.

The WHIP Program

The Wild Horse Inmate Training Program, or WHIP, benefits humans as well as horses by employing prison inmates as wild horse trainers. WHIP is a volunteer program. Under the supervision of master horse trainers, the inmates are taught to safely handle and train the mustangs. After being trained as riding horses, the mustangs are submitted to on-site BLM horse adoptions and sales. Wild horse training clinics are also offered at some of these events. WHIP facilities have untrained mustangs as well as trained mustangs available for adoption. Adopters must have a BLM-approved application and appropriate transportation.

The Canon City Wild Horse Inmate Program (in Colorado) has halter-trained, as well as saddle-trained, horses available for adoption. Horses are screened for trainability before going into the adoption program. Health guarantees are provided, and the facility has a return policy, though the BLM part of the fee is not refundable.

The facility also offers halter training for a reasonable fee to adopters of untrained mustangs. These inmate programs do a pretty good job of training horses. Some of the horses that emerge from prison programs are eventually used as therapy horses. As part of their Wild Horse Inmate Program, the Canon City facility trains and screens horses for the Assurance Home Mustang Project in Roswell, New Mexico. Working with horses is an important part of the therapy programs available for at-risk children at the Assurance Home. Contact information for the Caron City WHIP facility is listed in the appendix.

The Assurance Home Mustang Project

For over twenty-seven years, the Assurance Home, located in Roswell, New Mexico, has been taking in abused and neglected children from dysfunctional homes. As a part of the home's unique counseling and therapy program, at-risk children learn to work with horses. The children socialize, desensitize, and care for the horses with the eventual goal of producing gentle, quiet animals that are appropriate for therapy work. After the horses successfully graduate from the Assurance Home Mustang Project, they are passed on to other therapy programs.

According to project trainer and counselor Lee Kyser, the program's most important rule is that whatever task they are doing has to be a good, safe experience for both kids and horses.

The horses that the children work with are trained and screened first by personnel at the Canon City Wild Horse Inmate Program facility before they arrive at the Assurance Home. Kyser explains the transfer process: "The Wild Horse Inmate Program at Canon City does a really good job of screening the horses for us. We take some of the kids from the Assurance Home with us when we go up there to get the horses. The traveling is a lot of fun for them. They help us pick out some of the trained horses for our therapy program, from about three to ten that they will have saddled up for us. This is a good opportunity to teach the kids that a good disposition is much more important than a pretty color when you are choosing a horse for therapy work."

Once the horses arrive at the Assurance Home, they undergo a socialization process. Kyser describes this bonding phase, which is the first part of the Assurance Home training program: "The first thing we do with the horses when we get them back is bond with them. We offer them reassurance by loving them as much as possible. We do everything we can to make them feel secure and get them settled into their new home.

"Then we start the training phase. Part of this is teaching the children how to communicate with the horses, and how to earn the animal's trust and confidence. The children soon learn that if they violate that trust, it is hard to get it back—horses don't lie."

The children learn to understand equine body language and to observe the way their own behavior affects horses' behavior. They learn that when they behave in an aggressive manner, their body posture and movements will have a negative effect on horses' behavior, generating fear and mistrust. By paying closer attention to their own body language and the emotional cues they are giving off, the children learn to be more aware of how their behavior affects other creatures in their environment. By improving communication skills with horses, the children may eventually learn to apply this knowledge to relationships with their fellow human beings.

Always looking for opportunities to improve the children's coping skills, Kyser also makes a point of relating the mustangs' learning environment to some of the problems their young caretakers have to face. "A lot of life's lessons are learned during the mustang program. We discuss how the mustangs have been taken away from their environment, and now they are the children's responsibility. We talk about what the mustangs have to do to adapt to their new environment, how some of them waste a lot of time fighting, while others give up and start learning and make really great riding horses. We relate the mustangs' situation to the kids' situation."

Another important part of the Assurance Home Mustang Project is the desensitization process. Because the eventual goal of the training is to make good therapy horses, the animals have to learn to accept all kinds of strange new objects and situations calmly. The children expose the horses to wheelchairs and walkers so that they will react calmly when exposed to physically challenged people using such mobility aids. The children also desensitize the horses to other potentially disturbing stimuli such as balloons, lawn mowers, and noisemakers. Of course, the children are expertly supervised during this process, and the emphasis is always on safety.

Under the right supervision, working with horses can help children develop patience and a sense of responsibility. Riding also helps build confidence, as well as improving muscle coordination. The Assurance Home Mustang Project is helping many at-risk children learn skills they will need to succeed in later life, and children with disabilities all over the country are receiving the benefits of well-trained therapy horses from this facility. If you wish to help support this fine program, contact Ron Malone, Executive Director, at the following address:

Assurance Home
1000 East 18th Street
Roswell, NM 88201
www.assurancehome.org

The BLM Mustang Adoption Process

The Bureau of Land Management's Wild Horse and Burro Program oversees the adoption process for the wild horses and burros gathered from the public lands under its care. The adoption process begins with an application.

Applicants must be at least eighteen years old. Applicants are allowed to adopt as many as four horses in a twelve-month period. The applicant will be asked to state preferences for the age and sex of the horse being adopted.

Transportation and housing arrangements for the adopted horse must be specified on the application. The Bureau of Land Management has certain requirements for how an adopted mustang must be housed. Adequate shelter must be provided and must consist of some kind of permanent structure. Fences must be at least six feet high for horses over eighteen months. The space between fence rails cannot exceed twelve inches. Specific housing requirements may vary according to the rules of the administering BLM office for the part of the country where the adopted horse is to be housed.

Once completed, the adoption application must be mailed to the state Bureau of Land Management office serving the applicant's area for review. The Bureau of Land Management will contact the applicant once the application has been reviewed and approved. An inspector may come to the adopter's home to examine the facilities, either before or after the adoption.

Once the application has been approved, the applicant can adopt a horse from any one of many permanent adoption sites all over the country. Some of these permanent facilities offer trained horses and clinics to train the new owner. Horses can also be adopted from satellite adoption centers at scheduled special events. Adoption schedules can be acquired by calling the BLM office or visiting their Web site.

Applicants at special events should have an approved application in hand. The BLM also has very specific requirements as to what kind of trailer can be used to haul the mustang from the adoption site. Bureau personnel may not allow mustangs to be transported in two-horse trailers with dividers or ramps. Check regulations *before* you go to the holding facility. Adopters from out of state will also have to acquire a health certificate from a local veterinarian in order to transport a mustang across state lines.

General information on the BLM mustang and burro adoption program can be acquired from the Bureau of Land Management, National Wild Horse and Burro Program Web site, www.wildhorseand burro.blm.gov, by calling (866) 4MUSTANGS, or by writing the Bureau of Land Management, Attn. Wild Horse and Burro Program, 7450 Boston Boulevard, Springfield, VA 22153.

Giveaways, Sale Barns, and "Bargain" Horses

An owner who may no longer be able to keep a horse due to a crisis involving health or finances may be willing to part with the horse for little or nothing if assured the animal can find a good home. You can end up with a perfectly good companion animal if the previous owner was the conscientious type and an unexpected problem led to the frantic search to find a good home for a beloved horse.

Sometimes the search for a good home is complicated by the fact that the horse is over the age of fifteen years. Most people prefer to buy a younger animal, though older horses tend to be more patient with children and novices, are more reliable, and are usually easier to handle. An older horse can turn out to be the deal of a lifetime for the novice horseman, especially if the previous owner was conscientious about health care and training.

Unfortunately, the more likely scenario is the one in which the owner lost interest in the animal some time ago and inconvenience ended the relationship. Impulse buyers often purchase a horse without bothering to find out how to handle one first. If the greenhorn is lucky, the horse may turn out to be a good old boy who is willing to fill in for his owner's lack of knowledge—for a while. If the owner is unlucky, the horse may immediately decide to take advantage of his rider's ignorance.

Some horses do not suffer fools gladly and will promptly treat the inexperienced drugstore cowboy who thinks he knows it all to a backyard rodeo immediately after the first rough jerk on the reins. After a couple of wrecks, the owner may tire of his new toy. He will also find out that caring for horses is hard work, not to mention expensive. At this point, he may retire his cowboy hat to the attic and buy a leather jacket and a motorcycle. Motorcycles don't have minds of their own and follow their owner's directions, providing he or she knows how to operate one. The unwanted horse is subsequently relegated to a back pasture and a state of benign neglect. The animal may be well fed, but he probably hasn't been ridden for a few years.

The worst-case scenario is a half-starved nightmare whose hooves look like a pieces of driftwood found on the beach at low tide. The animal's backbone sticks up like a razor blade, and you could hang your hat on his hipbones. He staggers right up to you, big, brown eyes pleading for help. You now have a choice. You can turn your back on the whole mess and burn rubber getting to a phone to call your local animal welfare agency. Or, you can elect to rescue an endangered horse on your own. The fact that you're reading this book suggests you probably chose the second option, even though you knew better.

If you are a novice horse owner reading this book, we know you just couldn't leave that poor old horse there, in that awful place, with those horrible people, but please get yourself some expert help and advice. Otherwise, you or a family member might be injured, and the horse could suffer as well. I hope you will find the information in this book useful, but some things just can't be learned from a book.

Or maybe you are one of those "horse traders" who habitually fix up neglected horses, fatten them up, retrain them, and resell them to good homes. Although you are pretty good at doctoring and training, you are lucky to break even on any of your so-called "bargain horses," but that's okay because you enjoy fixing broken horses. Or maybe you are the operator of a horse rescue, and habitually go looking for this kind of trouble. Whatever the reason, may God bless you and keep you safe, and may you always win the good fight.

Sale Barn Rescues

Habitual sale barn horse traders can often be identified by their bronco-buster limps and beat-up horse trailers. Purchasing horses from low-end livestock sale barns is a risky business, even for so-called equine experts. Neophytes, especially animal lovers, should definitely avoid sale barns. Tenderhearted individuals may suddenly find themselves bidding against a horsemeat buyer to keep some poor old wreck from becoming dog kibble.

It is possible to attend horse sales and avoid temptation, though sale barn "bargain horses" are hard to resist. Some preparation is necessary. Before you go, take care to reassure all concerned parties, including friends and family members, that you have absolutely no intention of buying another horse. Emphasize the point by leaving your horse trailer at home. That way, you can wait around at the sale barn with your new purchase while a close friend or understanding spouse drives all the way back to the farm to fetch your rig.

Sale barns are good places to reflect on the insanity of having purchased yet another horse on impulse, especially an animal of indeterminate lineage, with possible health and safety issues. And just in case you run out of things to worry about, sale barn groupies, those retired old codgers that attend every horse sale just to watch the fun, will be happy to share a few words of wisdom. They will gleefully point out any suspicious lumps, bumps, or behavior peculiarities your new horse may exhibit, and they will keep you entertained for hours while you are waiting to be rescued.

Supporting Equine Rescue Organizations

Buyers for the horsemeat trade congregate at low-end livestock sales similar to the one previously described. "Killer" buyers generally pay $500 or less for the horses they purchase, since they figure their profit by the pound. If you wait until the end of a livestock sale, you may observe them loading their purchases into stock trailers. Young, untrained horses of indeterminate lineage, old horses past their prime, fat, furry little ponies, even mares with colts at their sides end up crammed into stock trailers designed to haul cattle. Some of the horses being loaded may have obvious injuries. A few will be so lame they can barely walk.

People who regard horses as livestock, as opposed to pets, see nothing wrong with making a few dollars in the horsemeat industry. Others regard the horsemeat trade as a necessary evil, and frequently voice concerns regarding the fate of the estimated 50,000 horses per year that would be dumped on low-end markets or abandoned in back pastures to die of neglect if horse slaughter were outlawed.

Be that as it may, whether homeless horses are regarded as companion animals, disposable livestock, or simply a logistics nightmare, they should not have to suffer needlessly. At the very least, legal efforts to make the shipping process more humane should be aggressively pursued, and existing laws actually enforced.

Horse slaughter is an emotionally charged issue for anyone who loves and values horses as companion animals. However, unwanted horses need help, not sympathy. Thousands of displaced horses will need good homes with responsible owners, especially if horse slaughter is eventually outlawed. Animal rescue facilities could very easily become overwhelmed, and most of these organizations are operating close to capacity right now.

Horse rescuers are breaking their backs and their hearts trying to save these animals, one horse at a time, but hard as they try, they can't save them all. Public support is desperately needed. Lip service won't pay the feed bills.

Well-meaning friends often advise rescuers not to waste money on animals that are incapable of rewarding their efforts, but the rewards of fixing broken horses are spiritual in nature, and busy schedules don't leave much time for regret. Even when the good fight is finally lost, horse rescuers still believe compassion is the truest expression of humanity and the best possible evidence of the evolution of the human spirit.

How to Help

Horse lovers who don't have the means to adopt or rescue horses on their own can still help by donating money, feed, or equipment to rescue organizations. They can also contribute their labor by fixing fences, grooming, feeding, and cleaning stalls. Those with training skills can donate some time preparing horses for adoption and volunteering as temporary foster families. Horse lovers with computer skills might donate some server space to technologically challenged rescuers trying to find homes for unwanted horses.

Many rescue organizations also have sponsorship programs. Contributors sponsor one of the horses living at a rescue organization and take responsibility for its financial needs. The sponsor can receive regular updates on the horse and may be allowed scheduled visits.

Call up a local rescue facility and ask what you can do to support their efforts. There is a list of equine rescue organizations at the end of this book for anyone interested in helping.

References and Sources of Additional Information

American Standardbred Adoption Program Web site: www.4the horses.com

Assurance Home Web site: www.assurancehome.org

Bureau of Land Management National Wild Horse and Burro Program Web site: www.wildhorseandburro.blm.gov

EARS Web site: www.foalrescue.com

ReRun, Inc. Web site: www.rerun.org

2

Caring for Rescue Horses

Any recently acquired horse may have health and safety issues of which the new owner is unaware, and a good pedigree is no guarantee that the horse has always been cared for by responsible people. Many of the horses currently living at rescue facilities have previously competed in the show ring or on the racetrack, only to narrowly escape death on the wrong side of the tracks. A little extra tender loving care may be required. The following chapter deals with basic horse care and common health problems. However, a veterinarian should always be consulted regarding health concerns, especially when dealing with a horse whose treatment history is unknown.

Homecoming: Immediate Concerns

Bringing home a new horse is exciting, especially for the horse that's bouncing around like a giant helium balloon at the end of a new owner's lead rope. If your recent purchase is doing cartwheels in his stall, congratulate yourself. There is a good possibility you just bought yourself a healthy horse. Worry about training issues later. You both need some time to settle down. A horse that appears dull and disinterested in new surroundings may be ill and should be watched closely for the next few hours.

If the horse has been on a long trailer ride, turn him out in a small pad-dock or round pen to stretch his legs a bit, and give him a chance to roll. But if he is highly agitated, it will probably be safer for the both of you to leave him in a quiet stall to settle down for the night. Horses are lovers of routine. Most of them will be upset by the sudden change in their envi-ronment. It can take weeks for some horses to adjust to a new home. Oth-ers settle down immediately, inspect their new quarters curiously, quietly munch some hay, and eventually lie down to rest for a while.

Despite what you may have heard, horses do not always prefer to sleep standing up. It is not unusual for a horse to lie down and sleep for a few hours, especially an exhausted horse. If he is still lying down the morning after you get him home and refuses to rise for food or anything else, then you have reason to be concerned. If he shows signs of pain, looks back at his flanks, or shows any other signs of discomfort, call the vet.

You can offer the horse a handful of grain, but no more than that, when he first arrives. His digestive system has already been stressed by the move, and too much grain can make him sick. The reasons for offering a bit of grain the first day are for reassurance and to check for health problems. A horse who refuses to eat the handful of grain may be ill. Make sure he has access to clean, fresh water, and salt. You can also offer him a flake of timothy or other good-quality grass hay. After he has had a couple of hours to settle down, the horse should show some interest in food or water. A horse that shows no interest in grain or some other treat, such as carrots or apples, may very well be developing serious health problems.

Dehydration

Water is especially important. Ideally, while traveling in a trailer a horse should be given a half-hour break every four hours, untied, and offered water. Unfortunately, not everyone who ships a horse is this conscientious. If you purchase a horse at a sale, the seller may have long-hauled the horse for many hours without any kind of break. Twenty-four-hour stretches are not unusual. Some horse traders routinely bring loads of horses to sale barns where meat buyers gather. They are not necessarily concerned about the condition of the animals once they get there. If you purchase a horse at one of these places, dehydration is a concern. If you have reason to suspect that the horse has been deprived of water for a long period of time and he will not drink, you can try putting a small amount of salt on his tongue or in the corner of his mouth to stimulate him to drink.

Signs of Dehydration

To test for dehydration, perform the pinch test. Pick up a fold of skin from the shoulder or neck area. It should spring back almost immediately. If the fold remains for several seconds, the horse could be seriously dehydrated, requiring veterinary care.

A dehydrated horse may be obviously weak, head hanging, and legs visibly trembling. Press your finger against the horse's gums. It shouldn't take more than three seconds for the color to return. The gums and tongue may feel dry and tacky. A heart rate of more than fifty beats per minute is another sign of trouble. Severe dehydration is a medical emergency. Call your veterinarian. The horse may have to receive a hydrating solution by nasogastric tube, or directly into the vein by catheter, in order to survive.

Treatment for Dehydration

You can offer a dehydrated horse an electrolyte solution flavored with apple juice or Kool-Aid, but he may not want to drink it. An electrolyte solution can be made by combining a potassium chloride salt substitute—such as No Salt—with plain table salt. Combine about a tablespoon of No Salt and a tablespoon of regular salt per gallon of water. Be sure you offer the electrolyte solution in a separate container from the plain water. Don't remove the plain water from the horse's stall. Always make sure he has access to clean, fresh water at all times.

Electrolytes can also be purchased in syringe paste form, much like worm medicine, but talk to a vet before giving a dehydrated horse any kind of concentrated electrolytes. Don't give a dehydrated horse dry electrolyte powder, as this can actually make the situation worse. A high concentration of undiluted electrolytes in a horse's stomach actually can pull water from the blood.

Pedialyte, a hydrating solution designed for human infants and available in any grocery store, worked well on a newborn colt belonging to one of the people involved with this book. The colt was born with a bacterial infection and became dehydrated as a result. The woman spent a couple of weeks pumping Pedialyte into the little guy, along with Peptol Bismol for continuing problems with diarrhea, the root cause of the dehydration. The upside was that with all the handling he received, the colt was halter broke and virtually bombproof before he was a week old.

The colt's owner used a large plastic dosing syringe to get the medicine into him by tipping his head up, inserting the tip in the corner of his mouth, and giving him time to swallow before administering the next dose. A bit of Karo syrup on the tip of the syringe helps a horse accept it.

Using Pedialyte would not be practical with a full-grown horse and would be somewhat expensive. Try mixing electrolytes into a warm, wet, oatmeal or bran mash to hydrate the horse. Make a bran mash by taking a scoop of wheat bran and adding enough warm water to make it juicy. You can also add pieces of apple and carrot. Most horses like the taste of bran mash, and many experienced horse people swear by the stuff.

Note: One of the reasons bran has fallen out of favor is its high phosphorus content. Both wheat bran and rice bran can be purchased with added calcium to offset the high phosphorus content. An advantage of feeding calcium-enriched or "stabilized" rice bran is its high fat content. Stabilized rice bran also does not go rancid as quickly as non-stabilized rice bran.

You can also replace some of the lost calcium and phosphorus in a dehydrated horse's system by offering a very small amount of alfalfa hay. Be careful about feeding alfalfa hay to a horse that isn't used to it, especially a debilitated horse.

Feeding a New Horse

The first day a new horse arrives, it's best not to feed it much grain. It is safest to just to provide some good grass hay, such as timothy or a clover mix. But if you choose to give him a little bit of grain as a treat for reassurance, don't give him more than a couple of handfuls. Be careful, especially if he is dangerously emaciated to the point where you can count his ribs, see his backbone, and see the bone structure of his hips. Too much grain can overload a starving horse's system, with lethal results.

You can safely feed a starved horse grass hay, as well as provide water and access to salt, when you first bring him home. However, rehabilitating a starved horse is not a job you should try to tackle without veterinary advice and assistance. Have a vet out as soon as possible. The horse will have to be on a special diet, and he may require emergency medical care to treat dehydration and other complications of malnutrition. Also, contact equine rescue organizations in your area and ask for help. You will be fighting the good fight, and will be in dire need of the advice and support of experienced people. There is a special section on page 40 on dealing with malnutrition. It includes diets and care advocated by experts, but you should follow your veterinarian's recommendations in order to return your horse to good health.

Assuming that the new horse has not been starved, he should be provided with some of his customary grain, so that changes in his diet can proceed slowly over the next few days by mixing his old grain mix with the new. If this is not possible, slowly increase his grain ration over the first few days. Feed two feedings per day. You can safely give him a half pound the second day at each feeding. Increase the amount by another half pound every three days. Most average-sized (around 1,000 pounds), lightly used horses don't require more than four to six pounds of grain per day, split into two feedings of two to three pounds each, morning and evening. A horse's digestive system works more efficiently when you split his rations into two or three feedings per day.

If you want to increase the horse's rations beyond four to six pounds, give more hay, not more grain. Giving a horse more than five pounds of grain at a single feeding is not healthy for his digestive system. A horse's digestive system was designed to process a high-fiber roughage diet, in small amounts, over a long period of time.

The rest of the horse's rations should be made up of about sixteen to twenty pounds of good hay per day. Give him plenty of good quality hay, but not more than 3 percent of his body weight in a single day. Most horses won't eat that much hay. You can adjust the quality of the horse's hay by mixing in a bit of alfalfa. Straight alfalfa is high in protein and phosphorus, so it must be introduced slowly into a horse's diet. A couple of pounds of alfalfa per day added to his grass hay should be sufficient. Be aware that alfalfa can be hard on the horse's system if he has certain medical conditions, such as kidney problems or a history of bladder and urinary tract stones.

If you are going to put the horse out on good pasture, you won't need to feed as much hay. The first time you put him out on pasture, only leave him out for two hours or less, unless you know for sure that he has been out on grass routinely before you bought him. If the horse isn't used to eating green grass, he may colic or founder. Be especially careful if the horse is severely underweight. If the horse has been starved, too much lush grass could overwhelm his digestive system. Talk to your vet before letting a starved horse out on lush grass for more than half an hour at a time.

If the horse needs to gain weight, you can add fat to his diet by mixing a bit of corn oil in with his grain. Start with a tablespoon at each feeding, and slowly work up to a half cup. You can add as much as two cups per day, but if your horse doesn't like the taste of corn oil, you would be sabotaging your own efforts. Try one of the high-fat, high-fiber feeds available from companies like Nutrena. Palatable high-fat food supplements for horses, some containing probiotics to aid digestion, can be also be added to a horse's feed. If your local feed store does not carry such items, they can be ordered from suppliers such as Valley Vet Supply at (800) 356–1005 or www.valleyvet.com, and Stateline Tack at (800) 228-9208 or www.statelinetack.com. Both give good, prompt service.

Scheduling a Veterinary Exam

Any horse with an unknown medical history needs to be scheduled for a veterinary exam to check for disease. You should also have him vaccinated as soon as possible. At minimum, he should be vaccinated for tetanus, Eastern and Western equine encephalomitis, equine influenza, and rhinopneumonitis. The West Nile vaccine is also a good investment, especially if you live near swampy areas.

Quarantine

A debilitated horse should never be turned out with healthy horses. He will be unable to defend himself. He may also be carrying a contagious disease that may infect others in the herd. Even if the new horse looks healthy, wait a few days before turning him out with other horses. Respiratory diseases such as shipping fever are highly contagious, and the stress of coming to a new home can lower the disease resistance of the healthiest horse. Feed and water the new horse separately for at least two weeks.

Welcome to the Pecking Order

Allow the new horse to investigate an unfamiliar pasture alone, at first. Give him plenty of time to scope out the premises during daylight hours. If you have electric wire fencing, there is a distinct possibility that the horse may not actually *see* the fence and may run right into it if he suddenly gets the idea that an imaginary pasture monster is chasing him. Attach white cloth strips, white tape, or some other visual aid around the perimeter.

Horses are social animals and require companionship, but horseplay can get rough!

Introduce the other horses slowly, preferably one at a time. Pick a good-weather day to introduce the horses to one another, in a safe area, with decent footing. Don't choose the day after a rain, when the pasture is muddy. Don't introduce strange horses near feeding time. Do it early in the day, so that you have several hours to observe their interactions.

Note: Rivalry among horses can get ugly. Horses have a pecking order and can be territorial with newcomers. Some new horses can blend seamlessly into any herd, but others give off all the wrong signals and will immediately get themselves into trouble. *continued*

continued

For instance, some ex-racehorses have been kept in isolation to prevent injury while on the track and may be unfamiliar with herd politics. Horses that have not been socialized with other horses may prove to be overly timid or aggressive in a herd situation.

Unusually timid horses might be chased right into a fence. Dominant horses may immediately proceed to fight their way up the chain of command. Injuries can happen. Have help available when you turn the new horse out with other horses the first time, as you may have to intervene if the herd gets too rowdy. Pay close attention to what is going on for the next few days, and be sure to inspect your horses' hides for suspicious-looking scrapes and cuts.

Note: In some cases, previously starved horses may become unusually violent, aggressive, and territorial with food. I once threw a small pile of hay into a pasture containing a previously starved horse. This particular horse fiercely guarded the hay from the other horses, despite the fact that he was surrounded by a pasture full of perfectly green grass. After a couple of months of being fed free-choice grass hay, the animal finally figured out that such theatrics were entirely unnecessary, since food would always be provided for him at his current home.

Aggressive pasture behavior can be controlled to a limited degree by moving horses to different pastures, but if a previously neglected horse displays food aggression toward humans, it must be dealt with as a training issue (see "Aggression" on page 138).

In some cases, geldings and mares may have to be kept separated. Though geldings are unable to breed, they may still behave aggressively toward mares. Very old and very young horses may also become victims of constant herd aggression.

Worming

Within a few days of bringing a new horse home, he should receive deworming medication. If you know a new horse's health history, it is a good idea to wait a couple of days before giving any kind of medication. This will give you more time to observe any health problems, and it will also give the horse's digestive system time to settle down. A severely debilitated or malnourished horse, should be examined by a veterinarian before administering deworming medicine.

If you have reason to suspect that the horse hasn't been wormed for a considerable length of time, the safest course of action might be to offer one of the milder wormers. Otherwise, it is actually possible to kill so many worms at once that the horse's system can be damaged. Pelleted wormers are available that are not as harsh as the paste form and are specifically designed to be given daily in the horse's feed. Pelleted wormers such as Strongid C are easy to administer; you just put a measured amount in the horse's feed each day. Most horses will eat it readily. Use the pellets for three weeks, and then follow up with a dose of a stronger medication such as ivermectin. It is necessary to rotate the type of deworming medicine you use. The little beasties you are trying to kill can develop a resistance to certain medications. Also, certain deworming medications are not effective against all species of worms.

You will need to worm your horse every two months. There are several different types of deworming medicine you can use. The following medications are often suggested for a rotation program.

Pyrantel tartrate and pyrantel pamoate (Strongid) are effective against large and small strongyles, pinworms, and roundworms, but are not as effective against bots. Two months after using a pyrantel paste, use ivermectin (Zimecterin), which will kill the bots. Try to schedule an ivermectin dose after the first frost to kill bots more effectively. Two months after the ivermectin dose, use benzimidazole or fenbendazole (Panacur). Or you can use one of the newer dewormers, such as moxidectin (Quest). Moxidectin is not recommended for young horses under the age of four months. It is a very effective medication, but you need to be careful with the dosage.

> **Note:** Most horses are pretty underwhelmed at the whole idea of being medicated. You can avoid training issues by adding a pelleted or liquid wormer to the horse's feed. However, most horses will benefit from an advance-and-retreat approach to worming. Instead of attacking the horse with the syringe, try gradually desensitizing the horse to the syringe before trying to medicate. Work around his face with the syringe, but don't touch him with it until he settles down and accepts the sight of the thing near his face. Next, stroke his face and muzzle with the syringe. When he accepts that, put a bit of sweet syrup on the syringe tip, and give him just a taste, by gently inserting the tip into the corner of his mouth. When he accepts that, go ahead and worm him. The horse will still not be happy with you when the medicine hits his tongue, but you will avoid some tantrums (yours and his) and probably get more of the medicine down if you take time to do some training.
>
>

Some horse owners will advise you to double up on the dosage of certain deworming medications. Don't let anyone talk you into doing anything that might endanger your horse, whose digestive system might be more sensitive than you suspect. Talk to your vet first.

Dealing with Malnutrition

Half the fun of owning horses is the sheer beauty of the animals, whether they're playing in the pasture, or resting quietly, their healthy coats glowing softly in the warm light of a well-kept barn. Most people just love to look at them. It's hard to understand why anyone would want to look at a thin, neglected horse. Unfortunately, not everyone who owns horses is responsible enough to feed them regularly. Some people will actually underfeed a horse to make the animal more manageable. Most self-respecting horse owners would quit riding altogether if they had to starve a horse to the point of weakness just to be able to stay in the saddle.

The sight of a starved horse is a hard thing for any caring horse person to take. You can see the individual vertebrae of his spine, which threaten to push through the skin of his back. You could hang your hat on his hipbones, and count each one of his ribs. His neck is thin and wasted, and his withers stand out like the fin of a shark. His coat is dull and rough. The behavior of a horse in this state is generally listless, and he has little interest in his surroundings.

Animal welfare personnel will tell you that the root cause of most instances of neglect is ignorance. When a horse is so horribly neglected that its life is in danger, animal control seizes the horse. Until the courts decide its fate, the horse is taken to a local rescue facility where hard-working, dedicated people care for its needs. Once there, the horse is generally provided with water, salt, and grass hay free-choice. A veterinary exam is scheduled for the following morning, or sooner if the animal is in really bad shape.

Though diets at rescue facilities vary, starved horses may be fed very small amounts of a complete feed designed for senior horses three or more times per day. The amount is slowly increased over the next few weeks. The horse is also provided with free-choice grass hay, water, and salt.

One reason for using senior feed in a program for starved horses is the ease with which senior feed can be made into a mash or soup with warm water, so that horses with bad teeth don't have problems chewing them. If necessary, these feeds can be diluted to soup consistency and fed with a syringe. Adding water to the feed can help to rehydrate a horse that has become dehydrated. Also, senior feed is processed for ease of digestion.

Talk to a vet before giving a starved horse any grain. The system of a horse suffering from malnutrition cannot handle the carbohydrate content of grain. Some rescue programs feed tiny amounts of grain, at frequent intervals, but the total amount is carefully monitored. Do not turn a starved horse out on grass for more than a half hour the first day. A starved horse must be reintroduced to grass slowly, increasing the time by half-hour increments: One half hour the first day, one hour the second day, and so on.

Note: Overfeeding or feeding a starved horse the wrong diet can have lethal results within a few days, leading to kidney, heart, and respiratory failure. The safest course of action for an inexperienced person responsible for the care of a starved horse is to provide the animal with grass hay, water, and salt, and seek veterinary assistance as fast as possible. A starved horse that shows no interest in food or his surroundings, or shows signs of dehydration, requires immediate veterinary care. Do not bed a starved horse on straw, as he may try to eat the bedding. Also, do not worm a starved horse until a veterinarian says it is safe to do so.

Signs of Illness

Vital Signs

It is a good idea to check a new horse's vital signs the morning after he arrives, or sooner if he shows signs of distress. A resting horse should have a heart rate below fifty beats per minute; respiration rate should be around twelve breaths per minute. A respiration rate greater than thirty breaths per minute in a quiet horse is cause for concern. His temperature should be around 100 degrees, plus or minus one degree.

Using a Stethoscope

A stethoscope is a handy thing to have in case of emergencies. Using a stethoscope is much easier than trying to take a horse's pulse manually. A stethoscope can provide critical information about what is going on in your horse's heart, lungs, and intestines, and it is much more sensitive than the naked human ear. A stethoscope can be obtained from a medical supply house or drugstore. You can also order one from Valley Vet Supply at (800) 356–1005. If you can't find a stethoscope, a blood pressure monitor can be adapted for the same purpose by removing the cuff.

You can hear a horse's heart sounds in the girth area behind the left elbow. Press the end of the stethoscope against his rib cage. When listening to the horse's heart you will hear a lub-dub sound. Each lub-dub counts as one beat. Your horse's heart rate should be below fifty beats per minute at rest.

You can check his respiration by positioning the bell of the stethoscope about six inches down from his throatlatch, on the midline of his throat. His respiration rate should be around twelve breaths per minute at rest. Then move to his chest area, and listen for any sign of congestion. Crackling, squeaking, or wheezing sounds may indicate lung problems.

You can also use a stethoscope to check your horse's gut sounds, by moving the bell of the stethoscope to his flank area. Be sure to check both sides for the healthy gurgling sounds that indicate everything is working correctly.

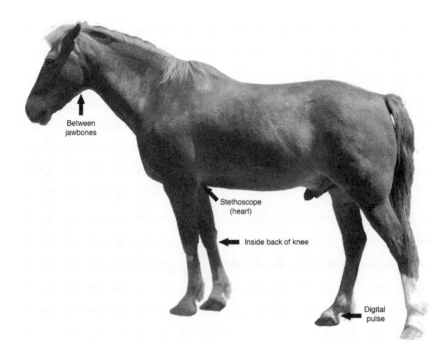

Between
jawbones

Stethoscope
(heart)

Inside back of knee

Digital
pulse

Heart and respiration rates will vary somewhat among individual horses. For instance, the normal vital signs of a young horse in good physical condition will differ from those of an older horse who is not as fit. You need to check your own horse's respiration rate when he's relaxing in his stall to use as a reference as to what is normal for him. If you have been exercising your horse, his heart and respiration rates should return to normal in about fifteen minutes.

If you don't own a stethoscope, you can take a horse's pulse manually anywhere a large artery lies close to the surface of the skin. Some of the easier areas to check are located under the left side of the jawbone, or the insides of the forelegs around the knee area where you can see the large arteries. Practice doing this before an emergency. Checking a horse's pulse takes a bit of skill! You can check a horse's respiration rate by watching his nostrils and rib cage expand and contract.

Capillary Refill Time

Lift your horse's upper lip and press on the gum until the color blanches out. Once you release the pressure, the color should return to normal within two seconds or less. If his gums are much paler than normal to begin with, you have a serious problem. Call the vet.

Taking a Horse's Temperature

Make sure you use a large-animal thermometer designed for the purpose. You can get one from your vet. Shake the thermometer down, coat the end with vaseline, and stand to the side of your horse. Move his tail aside and gently insert the thermometer into his anus about two inches and wait three minutes. Your horse's temperature should be 100 degrees Fahrenheit, plus or minus one degree.

Impaction Colic

Colic is always a danger with new horses due to stress and change of diet. Water deprivation also increases the risk of intestinal blockage, which causes a horse to colic. If the horse shows no interest in food of any kind, sweats, or looks around and kicks at his stomach, suspect colic. You may be able to see his abdominal muscles cramping. Press your ear to his flanks; you should hear gurgling and rumbling noises. Silence is an indicator of impaction colic. If the situation worsens, his heart rate will increase to more than fifty beats per minute, his gums will be pale, and he may roll and thrash around in pain. Colic is a medical emergency, and you should get immediate professional help from a veterinarian.

While you have your veterinarian on the phone, ask him if you can try administering some Banamine (flunixin meglumine) for the pain. Banamine is an anti-inflammatory pain medication that comes in a paste form (like worm medicine), or it can be administered as an injection and should be an essential part of any first-aid kit for horses. You can also try giving some mineral oil, which will help reduce the absorption of toxins and may even get his intestines moving again. Using a large plastic syringe or a small-mouthed plastic bottle, pour or squirt the oil into the side of the horse's mouth in the same area where the bit goes. Dosing with a bottle is messier but it helps if you tip the horse's head up a bit. Try to get at least a cup of oil down the horse if you can. If more oil ends up inside the horse than on your clothes, you are going pretty well. Be sure to tell the veterinarian of any medications you have given your horse as soon as he or she arrives.

Hand-walk the horse, and keep him on his feet until the vet arrives. Walking the horse will help evacuate the gas buildup that accompanies colic and, if you are really lucky, will get things moving again in his intestines. The horse may want to lie down and roll. Don't let him lie down at all if he is in intense pain and his movements are violent. But you can allow him to lie down for a couple of minutes and rest, providing he lies there quietly. Signs of recovery will include renewed interest in eating or drinking, and the evacuation of stools of normal consistency.

A healthy horse's nostrils should be clean and dry. White or colored mucus is a sign of trouble.

It is absolutely vital that horses have access to clean, fresh water at all times to guard against impaction colic. Use a tank or bucket heater in winter to keep water sources from freezing over. Horses prefer to drink cool, not cold, water. Eating snow is never an adequate winter substitute for clean, fresh water. Make sure the horse also has access to a clean salt block to encourage him to drink. If you have your feed custom mixed, you can also have 1 percent salt mixed into the horse's grain, along with providing a salt block.

A second type of colic, gaseous colic, has symptoms similar to impaction colic. However, the horse may have severe diarrhea, and the intestinal noises will be unusually loud. Gaseous colic is a medical emergency. Call the vet and ask if you can give the horse some Peptol Bismol to help the digestive system settle down and Banamine to ease the pain.

Respiratory Infections

If your new horse develops a cough, runny nose, and fever the day after you get him home, call the vet. Respiratory infections can develop into pneumonia. Keep the horse in warm, clean, dry quarters, and do not exercise him. Exercising a horse with a respiratory disease can do permanent damage to his lungs and delay recovery. Keep him isolated from your other horses for at least two to three weeks.

Shipping Fever

Everything from equine influenza to strangles has been referred to as shipping fever. However, the disease most commonly known as shipping fever is a form of bacterial pneumonia caused by dust and other foreign materials getting into the horse's lungs during transport. The bacteria that causes the inflammation is already in the horse's system. The stress of trailering lowers his immunity, and if the horse can't lower his head to evacuate dust and mucus effectively, the disease can get a foothold. A horse can come down with the disease the morning after you bring him home. Shipping fever has a very short incubation period.

The frustrating thing about shipping fever is that even an apparently healthy horse can develop it the morning after a short trailer ride. One of the people involved with this book had a healthy, bright-eyed mare delivered to her farm. The next morning the animal's nose started running. Shipping fever is highly contagious. Despite the fact that the rest of her horses were fed and watered separately, they all got the disease. Luckily, they had a mild form, and the sulfa pills the vet prescribed for the disease did the trick.

The long name for the sulfa pills is sulfamethoxazole-trimethoprim, an antibacterial agent often used to fight respiratory infections. If your vet prescribes sulfa pills to be given to your horse, the easiest way to give them is finely crushed and mixed with the horse's grain. You can crush them in a plastic bag and then add some sugar to help disguise the taste before mixing them into the horse's feed. An oral antibiotic paste, Tribissen 400, is administered by mouth syringe like deworming medicine, and it is often prescribed to treat respiratory infections, strangles, urogential infections, wound infections, and abscesses.

If sulfa pills or another form of oral antibacterial agent will not rid your horses of shipping fever, the vet may ask you to give the horse antibiotic injections. The safest place to give an injection is in the neck muscle. Some people may advise you to give shots in the chest, but don't do it. Blood circulation in the chest is poor.

Giving your own injections carries a certain amount of risk. You save money by doing your own injections, but you have to weigh the cost against that risk. Even if you decide not to take that risk, you may have to nurse your horse through a long illness and be required to give your own injections, because the vet can't be there all the time. Get training from a veterinarian or other qualified person before trying to give injections.

Equine Influenza

Equine influenza starts with a frequent cough and nasal discharge. Cloudy nasal discharge, especially if it has a yellow or greenish tinge, indicates a serious infection. The horse may appear sleepy or lethargic and may not have any interest in food. He will run a fever.

Call your vet. The virus may only last a couple of weeks, but a horse with equine influenza often develops pneumonia. Pneumonia can do permanent damage to your horse's respiratory system, or it may cost him his life. Do not attempt to ride your horse with the flu. The last time you had the flu you didn't feel much like exercising, and neither will your horse. Exercise can make his symptoms worse or cause a relapse and permanent lung damage.

Dealing with Injuries

Rescuing horses from the wrong side of the tracks may include dealing with some injuries the previous owner was either unwilling or unable to treat. Such people have been known to show up at fly-by-night sales with severely injured horses and even have the nerve to look puzzled when they are booed and harassed by other participants at the sale.

Old scars, lumps, and bumps may be harmless blemishes, or they may be evidence of chronic problems, especially in the presence of inflammation or lameness. All leg injuries should be regarded with deep suspicion, especially around the joints, coronet band, or heels. Old leg injuries, especially deep puncture wounds, can develop chronic abscesses. The bones, cartilage, and underlying structures may be involved. Some scars may require periodic treatment and removal of proud flesh. Proud flesh is a runaway overgrowth of granulated flesh on a wound due to infection and other complications. More information on leg injuries is available in the section on leg soundness on page 66.

Open wounds or recently healed wounds anywhere on the legs, especially around the joints, coronet bands, or heels, deserve special attention. Any large wound that penetrates the skin to the extent that muscle and other structures can be seen beneath, is unusually swollen, or appears to be infected should be examined by a vet. The vet will remove dead tissue and contaminants. Though open wounds are often sutured, if the injury is more than twelve hours old, the vet may decide against closure. Puncture wounds may have to be opened up in order to be adequately flushed and treated. The horse will also need a tetanus shot.

First Aid

Before the vet arrives, wounds can be flushed with a water hose on low pressure, or with a syringe filled with 10 percent Betadine and 90 percent water. Though slightly corrosive, 3 percent peroxide can also be used to flush a wound. After letting it bubble for a few seconds, peroxide can be quickly rinsed off with water to prevent tissue irritation. Peroxide can also be used in a dilute 1:1 solution with water.

An empty squeeze-type liquid dish-soap bottle, thoroughly cleaned and refilled with a Betadine or peroxide solution, works well for flushing out wounds. If the horse is being difficult, you can use the dish-soap bottle to flush out the wound from quite a distance. You can even open the stall door and gently flush out the wound while he is occupied with eating his grain.

Wounds that are bleeding heavily will flush themselves out. It is more important to stop the bleeding. To stop the bleeding, place gauze pads over the wound and press your hand firmly against the wound for several minutes. If the wound is on the leg, you can apply a pressure dressing. Cover the wound with gauze pads, wrap a gauze bandage around the leg, and cover with a stretch bandage. A wound that will not stop bleeding requires emergency veterinary treatment.

The vet will instruct the owner as to proper long-term care of the wound, which will probably include the application of antibiotic ointments and dressings. The owner may also be instructed to medicate the horse with oral antibiotics or even injections. The horse will have to be kept in a clean environment and away from flying insects until the wound heals.

Your vet may instruct you to keep the wound bandaged. Bandages protect wounds, especially leg wounds, from contamination. A gauze pad covered with an antibacterial ointment such as Fura-Zone can be placed over the wound, then a soft pad or disposable diaper wrapped around the leg, then an elastic bandage wrapped over that. Wrap the elastic bandage just tight enough to help hold the bandage in place, and then tape it in place. Inspect and change the bandage daily, and flush the injury with water.

Wound preparations that form protective barriers, such as Cut-Heal, often work well for long-term protection of partially healed, open wounds. Wipe the excess away from the skin surrounding the wound, and don't allow it to build up. Clean the wound daily by gentle hosing, or some other method, prior to applying the medicine.

Saddle Sores and Saddle Galls

Pressure injuries from ill-fitting saddles are called saddle sores. Saddle galls are swollen, painful pockets of serum often found in the wither area. Saddle sores and galls can become infected and may take weeks to heal. Ice packs can be used to reduce swelling and inflammation. Betadine solution can be used to flush open wounds. An antibacterial ointment and dressing can then be applied help heal and protect the injury. Zinc oxide ointment will soothe inflamed skin.

Evaluating General Health

Eyes

Eyes should be clear and bright. There shouldn't be any discharge running from them or swelling around the lids. If you see anything that looks suspicious, such as redness, foreign matter, pus, or a scratch on the surface of the eye, talk to a vet. A light-colored lozenge shape or cloudy area in the darker portions of the eye are also cause for concern and may indicate the presence of cataracts or the site of an old eye injury.

Eye injuries, including injuries to a horse's eyelids, require treatment. Equine eyes are fragile and will deteriorate rapidly if injuries are neglected. The horse's eye will not heal if a foreign body is embedded in the eye or trapped under the eyelid. Injuries left untreated

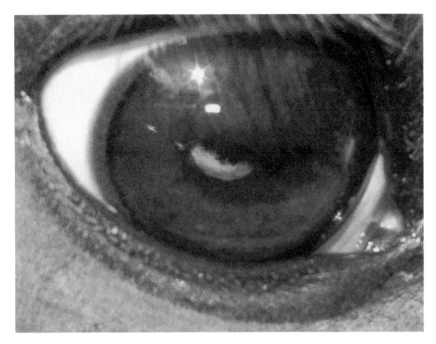

A whitish body in the eye may indicate a previous injury or the presence of a cataract.

will expose the eye to invasion by bacteria and fungi. The eye could ulcerate and the horse could go blind, even after long-term, expensive care. The injured eye might even have to be removed.

In cases where there is a lot of swelling around the eye, try a cold, wet compress to help reduce the swelling, or flush the eye with a syringe of water if the horse will let you. You can also take a clean washrag, wet it with cold water, gently place it over the horse's upper eyelid, and squeeze the washrag to allow the water to flow down into the horse's eye. Don't press on the horse's eye. If the vet can't come immediately, ask about administering a small dose of Banamine to help reduce the swelling. An injured eye will swell very fast, and permanent damage can be done if it isn't treated promptly. A good addition to any equine first-aid kit is an antibiotic ophthalmic ointment. Valley Vet Supply (800–356–1005) has a terramycin ointment that is good for pinkeye, corneal ulcers, and conjunctivitis in dogs, cats, and horses. You can also get antibiotic eye ointments from your vet. The best way to apply ointment to a horse's eye is to squeeze a line of it along the edge of a horse's upper eyelid. That way, the ointment will spread out over the horse's eye when he blinks.

Eyes that are running clear liquid, but don't appear painful or sensitive to bright light, may be caused by insect irritation. Invest in a fly mask, or let the horse out to graze during the night, when flies are not a problem. Dust can also irritate a horse's eyes. Mild conjunctivitis (eye irritation) can be treated by flushing the eye and using antibiotic ophthalmic ointment. If only one eye is running, and the horse shows no sign of pain, a blocked tear duct might be the problem. A blocked tear duct requires veterinary attention to correct it.

Uveitis, commonly known as moon blindness, is a chronic eye inflammation that causes blindness in horses. Symptoms vary, but they may include cloudy eyes, tearing, redness, and pain. The original cause may have been disease or injury, but the immune system of the horse continues to attack the eye tissue. Uveitis is generally considered to be incurable and chronic. The horse has to be under veterinary care for the remainder of his life. Corticosteroids are used to treat uveitis. They can be administered either by eye ointment or injection to help control inflammation and must be used under veterinary supervision. Bute and other anti-inflammatory drugs also help to control inflammation. Atropine drops and ointments are used to treat adhesions and contracted pupils. Antibiotics may be needed for secondary bacterial infections. Certain worm medications cannot be used during episodes of inflammation. If your horse is diagnosed with uveitis, talk to your vet before giving worm medications.

Recent advances in veterinary medicine have led to some hope for successful management of uveitis. In a new technique, a surgical implant delivers cyclosporin, a medication to prevent the harmful immune reaction that damages the eye tissue. E-mail inquiries about this new treatment can be directed to the Veterinary Teaching Hospital at North Carolina University at ophth@ncsu.edu. Their ophthalmology center is considered a leader in the field of equine opthalmology. They diagnose and treat other eye conditions as well, including cataracts, corneal ulcers, glaucoma, and tumors.

Teeth

There are a lot of good reasons to look in a horse's mouth before you buy him.

For one thing, you might want to make sure he actually has all of his teeth. Old horses eventually lose their molars (back teeth or cheek teeth). Some very experienced horse people have bought thin, neglected horses out of pity, only to find out during the first veterinary exam that the poor old things were missing all their back teeth, or the molars were so worn down as to be no longer functional.

Determining Age by Examining the Teeth

Aging horses by their teeth may not be an exact science. One of the people involved with this book begs to differ with claims about how easy it is to tell the age of a horse just by looking at dental markings. Judging by their teeth, her twelve- and fourteen-year-old geldings both appear to be around ten years old. Since she bought the horses when they were weanlings, she knows exactly how old they are.

Be that as it may, certain patterns of wear and markings on the incisors will give you a rough estimate of your horse's age. The incisors are the twelve teeth in the front of your horse's mouth. You will need a helper to hold the horse while you examine the animal's teeth. Peel the horse's lips back. You should see his incisor teeth and the side of his tongue. Looks like a gigantic wad of old bubble gum stuffed between dirty piano keys, doesn't it?

Now reach into the gap and pull his tongue out the side of his mouth. If you are lucky, he will open his mouth for you. Otherwise, stick your thumb in the interdental gap and pry his mouth open, while your helper grabs the horse's tongue and holds it to the side and out of the way. If your horse is a male, watch out for those canine teeth, which are located a couple of inches back from the incisors. If the canines are long and sharp, they will need to be trimmed.

Incisors

Look at the horse's bottom incisors, in the front of the horse's mouth. If all you see on the top surface of the horse's bottom incisors are dark (nearly black) cuplike markings, the horse trader that sold you the animal wasn't lying by much if he claimed the horse was four to six years old. If what you see are light tan markings, and there are two of them, the horse is probably eight to twelve years old. If all you see is one faint marking, and the tops of his teeth are fairly smooth, he's probably over twelve. (Note: This method is only intended as a way of getting a very rough estimate of a horse's age.)

Males of the species do not get their canine teeth until the age of five. The teeth of young horses are straighter in appearance when viewed from the side. The teeth of older horses appear to have more of a slant. They appear "long in the tooth," as the old saying goes.

Galvayne's groove, a dark groove located on the last upper incisor on each side of the horse's mouth, is supposed to appear when a horse is about twelve. By the time a horse is fifteen, the groove should extend halfway down the last incisor, starting from the gum line. By the time a horse is twenty years old, the groove should extend the full length of his tooth. By the age of twenty-five, the groove has retreated

Galvayne's groove is found on the third incisor. It appears at the age of twelve and completely recedes by the age of thirty.

from the gum line and extends halfway up from the bottom of the tooth. By the age of thirty, Galvayne's groove has disappeared.

Molars or Cheek Teeth

You will be unlikely to ever get a good look at your horse's molars without the aid of a speculum to hold the horse's mouth wide open and a flashlight. Molars are located too far back in the horse's mouth for casual examination.

You might want to carefully run a finger along the skin at the corner of your new horse's jaw, just to make sure he still has molars. No, don't panic yet, they're way, way, back there. Just keep looking.

Scheduling a Dental Appointment

Your new horse needs to have his teeth examined by a veterinarian or equine dentist. Even young horses need to have their teeth examined. Young horses are almost constantly losing their baby teeth and growing permanent teeth, until the age of five. Permanent teeth can erupt before baby teeth are shed, causing painful gum problems at the very time a colt is being trained to the bit. A trained professional can safely remove the baby teeth that are interfering with permanent growth. Also, a veterinarian or equine dentist can correct problems with a abnormal bite more easily if can you start regular dental care early, when the horse is a yearling if at all possible.

A veterinarian or equine dentist can float your horse's teeth, a term that refers to the process of grinding sharp edges off the teeth with a rasp or other tools. Wolf teeth can be removed, and overly long, sharp canine teeth can be trimmed.

Signs of Dental Problems

Dental problems can severely affect a horse's health. A horse that cannot chew his food properly may experience unexplained colic, choke, diarrhea, or failure to gain weight. Dental pain can cause behavioral problems such as head-tossing, resisting the bridle, or even bucking and rearing. A horse may become head shy and resist any attempts to handle his face or muzzle. A horse with dental problems will also behave strangely at feeding time, tilting his head at an angle while grain dribbles from the side of his mouth, or chewing up wads of hay and spitting them out again. Undigested feed may be observed in the animal's manure. He may show evidence of pain by tossing his head and suddenly jerking back from his bucket when trying to drink cold water. Other signs of dental problems may include excessive drooling, foul odor from the mouth, and cheek or jaw swelling and sensitivity.

If your horse stops eating and you suspect that the cause is dental pain, call your vet or an equine dentist. The horse's teeth will have to be attended to by a professional. In the meantime, ask the vet about giving the horse a dose of Banamine paste for the pain. This will probably make the horse comfortable enough to start eating again. Otherwise, you may have to soften his grain by soaking it in warm water. Hopefully, the horse will still be able to eat his hay. If the horse can't manage hay, let him out on pasture. If the horse's teeth are in such bad shape that he can't manage grass, switch him to a complete feed designed for senior horses, which can be softened with water to the consistency of soup if necessary.

Types of Dental Problems

Dental caps are baby teeth that do not shed before permanent teeth erupt past the gum line. If you examine your young horse's incisors and can see a definite demarcation between a permanent tooth erupting and a deciduous tooth (baby tooth), call your vet or equine dentist to have the old tooth removed. Dental caps can interfere with the growth of the permanent tooth, resulting in impactions and crooked permanent teeth. Dental caps can also fragment and cause painful injuries to the horse's mouth.

Parrot mouth is a term used to describe a horse with an overbite. Sow mouth is a term used to describe a horse with an underbite. A normal horse's incisors should meet in the middle. Horses with birth defects such as parrot mouth or sow mouth will require conscientious attention to dental care. The teeth of a horse will grow overly long any time there are no opposing teeth to wear them down. A horse with an overbite will need to have his incisors shortened to keep the lower incisors from hitting the palate and causing injuries, and to compensate for lack of wear from opposing teeth. Horses with an underbite deformity will also need to have their incisors shortened for similar reasons. Both kinds of bite deformity will also result in the formation of dental hooks.

Dental hooks and sharp molars are dental malformations caused by uneven wear at the tops of a horse's teeth. Uneven wear is generally caused by a bite deformity. Another contributing factor may be related to diet. Horses in the wild can spend more than twelve hours per day grazing, wearing down their teeth in the process. A stalled horse may spend only a couple of hours a day finishing up his hay and grain. But even if a horse spends most of the day outside grazing, sharp edges can develop along the edges of his molars. These sharp edges will appear along the outsides of the upper jaw teeth and the insides of the lower set. If these sharp edges get long enough, they will result in unnatural jaw movement when a horse chews his food, leading to the formation of dental hooks. Dental hooks form on the first molars on each side of the horse's upper jaw, like sharp little spikes pointing downward. These malformations in a horse's mouth can lacerate a horse's cheeks, causing pain and resistance to the bit.

Wolf teeth are vestigial premolars located on a horse's upper jaws in front of the cheek teeth, as in the photo below. Wolf teeth serve no useful purpose in a horse's mouth, and are leftovers from the prehistoric past. They can cause impactions by interfering with the growth of the rest of the molars. Because wolf teeth are located in front of the molars, they are in a position to cause bitting problems. The bit may press against them and cause the horse consider-

Canine teeth and wolf teeth are often confused. Canine teeth are located behind the front incisors. Wolf teeth are found in front of the back molars.

able pain. It is advisable to have wolf teeth removed by a veterinarian if they are present.

Canine Teeth are located a couple of inches back from the incisors, on the upper and lower jaws of a male horse. Though canine teeth are generally found in male horses, some mares also have very small canines. Canines can get very long and sharp, and they often need to be trimmed.

Skin and Coat

The coat of a healthy horse should be short and glossy during the summer months. When clean and brushed, body hair should lie down smoothly on the horse's back. Hair that lays in tufts and ridges may be a sign of impending skin trouble. An unusually long, shaggy, dull coat may be an indicator of systemic disease, poor nutrition, or worm infestation. Part the hair and take a close look at the surface of the skin. The presence of dandruff and flaky, scaly skin, or scabs and bumps, are signs of developing skin problems.

Common Skin Diseases

Equine dermatitis can result from bacterial or fungal infections, allergic reactions, or systemic problem. Any skin problem that does not improve within a few days should be brought to the attention of a veterinarian. The veterinarian will take a skin scraping for analysis to determine the exact cause of your horse's dermatitis.

> **Note:** For small patches of dry skin problems on a horse's body and legs, 20 percent ichthammol salve works well, and can be used with or without a dressing. Ichthammol is also used on human skin and is a mild treatment, though the stuff looks and smells pretty nasty. Ichthammol drawing salve is available from Stateline Tack at (800) 228-9208.
>
>

Rain Rot

A coat that stands up in tufts and ridges on the horse's back and the presence of flaky, scaly dandruff, especially along the topline and rump, are signs of the bacterial infection known as rain rot. Rain rot (dermatophilosis) is caused by the same bacteria responsible for the skin disease known as scratches, or mud fever, a scaly infection that appears on the lower part of the horse's legs around the pastern area, where the hair is long. If you examine your horse's skin closely, you will find scales and scabby, matted crusts of hair. When the infection is first getting started, you may feel the heat of skin inflammation when your horse first comes out of the rain and feel bumps starting under his coat. When you touch him on his back or rump area, he may flinch in pain.

Rain rot generally makes an appearance during a period of several consecutive days of wet weather. Rain rot thrives in moist and dirty conditions. Horses won't always come in out of the rain long enough to dry off, even when shelter is provided. When horses are kept outside during cold, wet weather and it is not practical to bathe them, it is a good idea to bring them in, dry them out completely, and brush them thoroughly, at least two or three times per week. Continuously wet conditions can damage a horse's skin, allowing the rain-rot bacteria to penetrate far enough to do damage. The best measures to prevent rain rot are cleanliness and frequent brushing. Rain rot is contagious by contact with an infected horse and with the infected horse's tack, blankets, and brushes.

Treatment: Since ointments and creams keep the skin surface wet, and rain rot thrives in wet environments, ointments are not the best choice to treat it. Antibacterial ointments might do some good, but they can also help spread the disease on the horse's skin. Instead, apply a topical antiseptic solution such as povidone iodine, or Betadine. Betadine solution can be sprayed on twice a week and can be used along with medicated shampoos. Iodine- or Betadine-based shampoos for horses work well. Iodine-based shampoos for dogs will also help. Wash the horse with regular shampoo first to get his skin clean before you use the medicated shampoo. As a general rule, medicated shampoos don't clean as well as regular shampoo. Leave the Betadine-based shampoo on the area to soak for about ten minutes before rinsing it out. Cider vinegar can also be applied to a horse's skin and has been reported to have healing properties.

Keep the infected area dry. With treatment and good care, the disease should start to improve within a few days. If it doesn't, call your veterinarian. Your horse may have developed a secondary bacterial infection and will require antibiotic injections to get better. Your veterinarian will take a skin scraping at that time to determine the exact cause of your horse's skin condition.

> **Note:** One cup of Absorbine veterinary liniment added to a five-gallon bucket of warm water makes a soothing antifungal body wash and helps heal conditions such as rain rot.

Ringworm

Ringworm is a common fungal infection. It is contagious and zoonotic, which means that it can be passed on to humans. Your cats and dogs can also get infected, along with your other horses. Keep the infected horse, his tack, blankets, and brushes away from the other horses. Disinfect everything that comes in contact with the infected horse.

The symptoms of ringworm are circular patches of hair loss. The lesions look red and inflamed at the margins. The skin is crusted and scaly. Ringworm lesions may be itchy and painful, causing the horse to flinch when you touch them.

Treatment: Wash the horse with regular shampoo to get him clean. Then use an over-the-counter Betadine- or iodine-based shampoo to get rid of the ringworm. Spray with Betadine solution twice weekly. Antifungal ointments such as Lotrimin and Tinactin can also help heal ringworm.

Allergies

Some insecticides can cause allergic reactions in horses. One of the people involved with this book had a problem with an insecticide when her horse's skin became irritated as a result of exposure to the fly-spray product. The animal's skin started flaking on the neck and chest areas. Once she rinsed the residual spray off their coats and stopped using that particular brand, skin problems resolved within a few days. The spray she had been using had a higher concentration of certain chemicals than the one she had been previously using. It is advisable to always follow the directions on fly-spray bottles, and be careful not to soak the skin.

I would never suggest that anyone stop using any fly spray products, especially if a horse displays symptoms of hypersensitivity to insect bites. Some horses are so allergic to insect bites that they will develop a scaly rash over their entire bodies. If insect hypersensitivity is a problem, horses can be kept inside during the day when biting insects are most active. Fly masks and sheets can be used when the horse is outside. Topical insecticides can be applied as well, but be careful to follow instructions and do not wet the skin.

Insecticides, insect bites, certain dewormers, foods, feed supplements, vaccines, and other medications can cause allergic reactions in horses. Hives are large, raised swellings or bumps on a horse's skin caused by an allergic reaction to something in the environment. The swellings are generally found on the chest, shoulder, and neck areas, though they may be dispersed around the entire body. They may be pruritic (itchy) or not.

Treatment: If you suspect that your horse is experiencing an allergic reaction, call the vet. He or she can run tests to determine if the horse's skin problem is the result of an allergic reaction. Skin allergies are generally treated with antihistamines and corticosteroids.

Warts

Warts are caused by a virus and can be spread by contact with other horses. They are generally present around the muzzle, but they are occasionally found on the legs. Warts inside a horse's ears are referred to as aural plaques.

Treatment: Talk to your vet before trying any home remedies for warts. Warts can be removed by freeze-burning with liquid nitrogen, or can be chemically removed with a topical preparation, but they may return to the same area. Benign neglect is often the best approach, as warts may disappear spontaneously after a few months. Putting anything in a horse's ears to remove aural plaques is not a good idea. Aural plaques may not be aesthetically pleasing to look at, but they are normally harmless to the horse's health.

Evaluating General Soundness

Conformation relates to soundness, but it is often evaluated according to breed preferences. An Arabian horse's dished profile is attractive, but since you don't ride a horse's head, such considerations are purely a matter of taste. Small ears may look neat, but what goes on between those ears is the most important thing. Some of the most sweet-natured, willing horses you'll ever meet have ears like mules and heads shaped like coal buckets.

According to some horse experts, the small, graceful-looking feet preferred in halter classes may be inadequate to support a horse's weight and prone to disease. On the other hand, mustangs often have very small feet, and mustangs are not known for having soundness issues.

Reality often circumvents common beliefs regarding the way conformation affects soundness. Triple Crown winner Secretariat had mild knock-knees, and the legendary Seabiscuit had mildly offset knees, both faults that theoretically have a negative effect on running ability. Cow hocks and angular (sickle) hocks are also frowned upon, yet many top cow horses display those particular conformation flaws.

Conformation flaws may be indicators of future durability, but a horse's performance also depends on factors such as heart, pain tolerance, and a patient, willing attitude. The following section will touch on conformation flaws that may cause soundness issues, though mild conformation flaws are unlikely to cause problems for the average owner of a lightly used pleasure horse.

Neck Soundness

A horse should be flexible in his neck. You should be able to bend his head and neck around easily on both sides without the horse moving his legs. A stiff neck may signal the possibility of spinal problems. A horse with a stress fracture or other injury to the cervical vertebrae will demonstrate neck stiffness when you try to turn him. Injuries of the cervical (neck) vertebrae can cause front-leg lameness.

You can also do "carrot stretches" with the horse to test his neck flexibility. Hold a carrot just out of his reach over the fence or stall door to see how far he can stretch to get it, or hold a carrot between his front legs, below and behind his knees, to see if he can reach down to get it easily. (The last exercise is also a good way to start teaching a horse to bow.)

Back Soundness

Take the eraser end of a pencil or pen and gently probe down the length of the horse's spine, on both sides. He should react by twitching his skin as though bothered by a fly. Numb spots may signal a neurological problem.

Check for back injuries. Gently but firmly press down with your fingers on both sides of the spine and check for sore spots. Also check the girth area. Press down lightly on the skin from withers to elbow. Soreness in the girth area may also be a symptom of back problems. Walk the horse in tight circles in both directions. He should move easily, without tripping or stumbling. Watch to see if he is reluctant to put weight on any of his feet. Walk him up- and downhill, with his head elevated, and watch for anything peculiar in his gait.

Poor back conformation will cause problems with getting a saddle to fit properly. Saddles may not stay in place as well on horses with down-sloping backs. Down-sloping backs have croups higher than the withers. Finding saddles for swaybacked horses and horses with unusually short, wide backs will also require more effort. A badly fitting saddle can cause saddle sores, pressure bumps, and soft tissue injuries that can require months to heal.

Symptoms of Back Problems

A horse suffering from back pain may exhibit the following symptoms: He may not want to hold his leg up for the farrier. While being saddled, he may be fidgety, swish his tail irritably, lay his ears back, and threaten to bite. A horse with a sore back may also dip his back when weight is put in the saddle.

The horse may sink down while being mounted. While being ridden, he may have trouble going up and down hills and will try to descend sideways. Body stiffness may be noted while turning. The horse may canter on one lead with no difficulty, but stumble and stiffen on the other. Gaits may become short and choppy. Back pain has been reported to cause extreme resistance, such as bucking and rearing, though it is also just as likely that the horse would be too stiff for such violent gymnastics.

Types of Back Unsoundness

Types of back unsoundness include muscle strains, ligament injuries, and spinal problems. Soft muscle injuries, such as muscle strains, are often the easiest to treat, and may disappear entirely after a few weeks of rest. More serious injuries, such as damage to the main ligaments adjacent to the spinal cord, can take months to heal. Spinal unsoundness, such as spinal impingement or "kissing spine," formation of bone spurs, and stress fractures can develop into a source of chronic pain and become a management problem for the remainder of the horse's life.

Treatment

If you suspect that your horse is experiencing back pain, call your vet. He can provide anti-inflammatory medications, such as phenylbutazone (bute), and muscle relaxants to help your horse heal. Rest and medication may be all your horse requires in order to recover. Corticosteriod injections may help to relieve the pain and inflammation accompanying spinal problems.

A new treatment for equine back injuries, known as ESWT (extracorporeal shock wave therapy) has been used in the past to treat tennis elbow and other musculoskeletal disorders in humans. ESWT has been shown to stimulate bone growth and help heal fractures. Injuries that have reportedly been treated successfully with ESWT include impingement of the dorsal spinous processes or "kissing spines," sore back muscles, suspensory injuries, bucked shins, bowed tendons, bone spavin, splints, maladaptive bone disease, ringbone, and navicular disease. ESWT therapy is currently in use in such facilities as Tufts Veterinary School in Massachusetts and the Purdue University Veterinary School in West Lafayette, Indiana. The Purdue facility has a high-energy focused shockwave device that can be used on standing, sedated horses on an outpatient basis.

Chiropractic Care and Massage Therapy

Chiropractic care has been reported to have beneficial results in some instances of chronic back problems. However, you should consult a veterinarian first and get his or her advice. Barehanded treatment is the safest form of chiropractic therapy. Do not allow a chiropractor to use rough methods involving hammers or other implements on your horse's back. Massage therapy can also be beneficial by relieving muscle tension and increasing blood circulation to the area.

Leg Soundness

While the horse is standing quietly, examine the legs from all sides. Look for any suspicious lumps or bumps. Feel the legs for heat, swelling, or sore spots. Watch the way a horse stands while at rest. If he stands with one leg habitually in front of the other, as though to transfer weight to that side, he may have a lameness problem.

Testing for Lameness

While you are leading the horse at a walk, have someone observe how he moves. Mild lameness may not show up at a walk. Trot the horse on a lunge line or in a round pen. Trot in both directions. Head nodding, especially at a trot, is a definite sign of lameness in the front legs. Watch him from the rear as he moves, and note whether he carries one hip lower than the other. Walk and trot him across a surface that will show tracks. Examine the tracks for signs of irregular movement.

The Flexion Test

The flexion test is a traditional soundness test. You can perform the flexion test on your horse by picking up each foot, bending the leg up under him, and holding it there for at least sixty seconds. Then release the leg and immediately trot him off. Many sound horses will show a positive result and limp slightly for a couple of steps before resuming a normal gait. An unsound horse will continue to exhibit lameness.

Dealing with Lameness

Tendon and ligament injuries occur when the legs are stressed. Hard training combined with poor conditioning, or rushing a young horse into training before his bones and tendons are fully developed, can easily result in strains and sprains. Extreme horse sports, such as racing, jumping, or barrel racing, may increase the risk of injury, but even a sedentary lifestyle is no guarantee of safety. Pasture potatoes can also damage themselves on a lazy afternoon when turned out to play with their buddies.

Lameness is cause for examination by a vet, especially if accompanied by heat and swelling. Correct treatment during the acute phase of a tendon or ligament strain will greatly reduce the damage caused by inflammation, which can result in chronic lameness problems. The horse should be confined to his stall. The injury can be hosed with cold water two or more times per day, for fifteen minutes each time, to reduce inflammation.

The topical anti-inflammatory DMSO is often recommended for tendon injuries, but talk to your vet before using it. DMSO can carry contaminants past the skin barrier, as well as making fresh bruises worse.

Cold-packing an injury is also an effective way to reduce inflammation. Crushed ice in a plastic bag conforms to the shape of a horse's leg. Do not apply the ice bag directly to the surface of a horse's bare skin. Use a layer of cloth or cotton for protection, or insert a bag of loose, crushed ice into an extra-long athletic sock and the sock can be tied loosely or otherwise secured to the affected area. Do not leave ice on a horse's leg for an extended period of time, but you can ice the leg several times per day. Special ice boots are available from suppliers such as Valley Vet Supply (800–356–1005). These ice boots are easy to apply with pockets for reusable ice packs and Velcro closures.

Pressure bandages will help to support the leg and reduce swelling, but don't wrap your horse's leg unless you know how to do it properly. A too-tight bandage can damage the horse's tendons. Get a vet or other qualified person to show you how. Leg quilts, sheet cotton, or other type of padding must be placed between the horse's leg and the bandage. Wrap from front to back, outside to inside. Tighten the bandage on the bone at the front of the horse's leg, not on the back where the tendon is located. Overlap the bandages as you wrap the injury.

All-in-one leg wraps, complete with pillow wraps and standing wrap material, can be obtained from suppliers such as Valley Vet Supply at (800) 356–1005. Horse Health USA (800) 321–0235 carries standing leg wraps with Velcro closures that are easy to apply, as well as other bandaging materials, and has a fast, dependable delivery service.

Anti-inflammatory drugs, such as bute or Banamine, will help with inflammation, but ask your vet before administering these drugs, especially if you are expecting his call that day. Anti-inflammatory drugs can mask symptoms and make an accurate diagnosis of your horse's problem more difficult. Your vet may recommend ultrasonographic and radiographic examination of your horse's injury, a period of stall confinement, and controlled exercise at a later date.

Tendon Injuries

Bowed Tendon

A bowed tendon is an injury of the superficial digital tendon running along the back of a horse's leg, from knee to pastern, or hock to pastern (see the photo below). A tendon is made up of bundles of fibrous tissue connecting muscle to bone. When injured, the tendon fibers can tear. The tendon becomes inflamed and swells, resulting in the characteristic "bowed" appearance on the back of the lower leg, and the horse goes lame. Bowed tendons most often occur in the back, mid-cannon area of the lower front legs. Symptoms of a bowed tendon are heat, swelling, and lameness. Both tendons and ligaments may be involved.

A bowed tendon generally starts out as tendonitis. Tendonitis refers to inflammation within the tendon. Symptoms of tendonitis are heat and swelling. Though the horse may not go lame with tendonitis, heat in the tendon area should never be ignored. Without proper rest and management, the fibers of the inflamed tendon will weaken and tear. Chronic injury can result in a bowed tendon.

Treatment: Confine your horse to stable rest and call your vet. He will probably recommend that you apply ice packs or hose the injury with cold water to control inflammation. Ask him if you should give

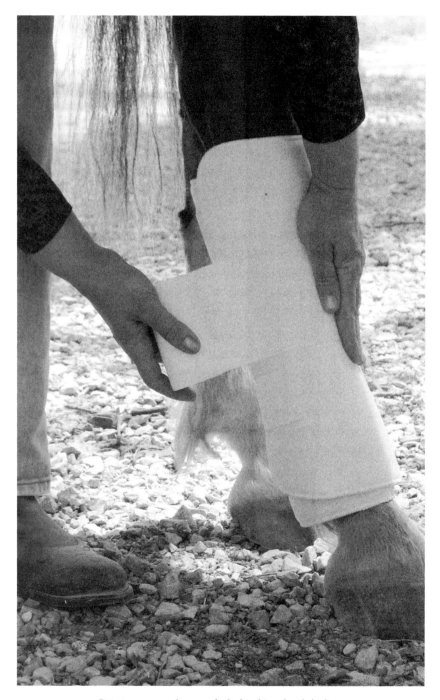

Pressure wrapping can help heal tendon injuries.

the horse anti-inflammatory medications, such as phenylbutazone or Banamine. Both are available in paste or liquid form.

After the initial acute phase of pain and inflammation (around forty-eight hours), alternating cold therapy with heat therapy is beneficial to help increase blood circulation to the area. Heat therapy can be applied by adding plastic wrap between the pressure wrap and padding, or over the pressure wrap.

Veterinary treatment for bowed tendon injuries may include injections of hyaluronic acid or short-acting corticosteroids to help control inflammation. Your vet will also recommend a period of stall confinement. During this period of stall confinement, the horse will need periods of controlled exercise, such as hand-walking, but he can't be ridden or turned out with other horses.

If more conservative treatments don't work, surgery may be recommended. The annular ligament may have to be severed so that the tendon can move more freely. Another common surgical procedure, tendon splitting, helps to drain blood and unwanted inflammation products from the tendon core.

Tenosynovitis

Tenosynovitis is an inflammation of the tendon sheath surrounding the tendon. Symptoms are similar to tendonitis and include heat, swelling, and lameness. The treatment is also similar, except that corticosteroid injections are used more often in the treatment of tenosynovitis. Antibiotics may also be prescribed when tenosynovitis is caused by a bacterial infection.

Tenosynovitis doesn't always result in lameness. In some cases, the buildup of fluid from an injured tendon sheath results in a harmless blemish after the initial inflammation subsides. Thoroughpin is a swelling of the deep digital flexor tendon sheath, and appears as a large, soft bump on the outside of the hock. Thoroughpin doesn't generally cause lameness or soreness, though it may be a symptom of deeper problems. In most cases, thoroughpin doesn't require treatment, unless for cosmetic purposes. Wind puffs are soft, mushy

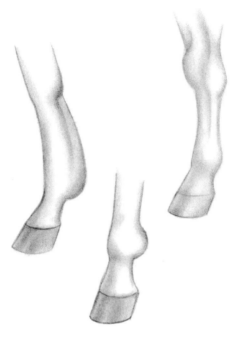

Tendon injuries

bumps around a horse's fetlocks (see the illustration above), and they don't usually cause problems unless they become large enough to restrict a horse's movement. Thoroughpin and Wind puffs are just the result of a buildup of fluid and shouldn't cause the horse any pain.

Ligaments, Bones, and Joints

Ligaments connect bone to bone. Ligament injuries are most common in the front legs, where a horse carries most of his weight. A mildly sprained ligament can result in pain, stiffness, and swelling, but it will respond to rest and a support bandage. Severe ligament injuries may require a cast and prolonged rest. Ligament damage can result in joint damage and chronic lameness, so good care and veterinary monitoring is vital. Ligaments support and stabilize joints, so ligament injuries often lead to joint problems if an injured horse is not rested and cared for properly.

Treatment: Contact your vet, and follow his recommendations. Treatment of ligament injuries is similar to that for tendon injuries, including cold therapy during the acute stage, anti-inflammatory medications, support bandages, stall rest, and controlled exercise. Ultrasonographic monitoring may also be recommended, as well as x-rays to check for possible bone fractures and other joint injuries.

Stifle Problems:
Upward Fixation of the Patella

A horse is said to be "stifled" when the patellar ligament locks over the end of the femur of the stifle joint, causing little actual pain, but a peculiar form of lameness. With mild stifle problems, the ligament will catch temporarily on the bone, and then the back leg will suddenly flip up toward the horse's stomach as though released from a tightly wound spring.

When stifle problems are severe, you may notice that the horse balks in the morning when you try to remove him from his stall. One of his back legs will be locked in the extended position. The back leg will be stiff, and the horse will be unable to bend it in order to walk normally. The horse will drag the back leg behind him and the toe will be dragging the ground (see the illustration below). If you back him up,

A ligament catches on the femur bone, locking in the extended position and causing upward fixation of the patella.

the leg will probably unlock. You may also need to massage and work the ligament areas for some time. Hopefully, the horse will then be able to flex it back up underneath himself and move somewhat normally. There will be faint popping and cracking noises as the joints flex.

Treatment: Talk to your vet. In some cases, exercise programs can help. Oral supplements such as MSM, hyaluronic acid, chondroitin sulfate, and glucosamine may be beneficial in maintaining joint flexibility.

If non-invasive therapies don't work, severing the medial patellar ligament is one of the most common procedures for dealing with a stifled horse. The surgery will immediately correct the problem. Many horses recover from surgery in a couple of weeks, but some take as long as a month to get over the soreness. Discuss any concerns you may have about complications of surgery with your vet, and do not resume normal activities with your horse until the vet gives permission. Some of the problems associated with this surgery may be due to the fact that owners don't allow their horses time enough to heal.

Knee Sprains

Symptoms of knee sprain are lameness along with swelling and stiffness. Knee swellings should be examined by a vet and x-rayed to determine if there is a fracture along with soft tissue damage. Bone chips can also cause chronic problems. Since knee ligaments keep the knee joint stabilized, the horse must be rested for as long as the vet recommends; otherwise the joint can be permanently damaged.

Curb

Curb results when the plantar ligament in the back of the hock is strained, resulting in inflammation. Symptoms are an obvious swelling that starts about an inch down from the point of the hock (see the illustration on page 76). The swelling is hard, not soft and fluid-filled. When the injury is new, there will be a lot of heat and swelling, along with lameness. Call your vet. Curb injuries, like any ligament injury, may take months to heal. However, with proper treatment, curb injuries generally stabilize and cause no further problems, though a permanent blemish will remain. Treatment is similar to other ligament injuries, including cold therapy, confinement, and anti-inflammatory medications. Several weeks of rest from training may also be recommended.

Suspensory Ligament Sprains

The suspensory ligament is located in the rear of the cannon bone and extends downward to provide support to the fetlocks. Symptoms of suspensory ligament strain are swelling around the back of the cannon and fetlock area and lameness. Fetlock sprains, especially those accompanied by swelling and lameness, may involve the joints and ligaments and should never be ignored.

Mild inflammation of the suspensory ligament may result in a chronic lameness that comes and goes mysteriously. A chronic inflammation can sometimes be detected by trotting the horse in a circle with the suspect limb on the outside of the circle or by performing a flexion test.

Even a mild case of suspensory ligament inflammation should be taken seriously, as it can deteriorate into a chronic condition known as degenerative suspensory ligament desmitis and cause permanent disability. The ligament will no longer support the fetlock adequately, resulting in lameness and a "coon-footed" appearance (see the illustration below).

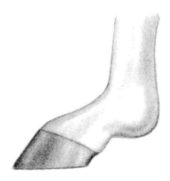

Dropped fetlock

Joint Problems

Joint problems can result from ligament injuries or from a direct trauma injury such as a fracture. Ligament damage causes joint inflammation by destabilizing the joint. Since ligaments are attached to bone, injury results in tearing of the connective tissue covering the bone. The injured bone covering will form a fibrous scar tissue and finally calcify. This new bone material wears away at the cartilage, and constant inflammation also damages cartilage. Damaged cartilage is replaced by new bone growth in places where bone wasn't meant to be, causing pain, joint stiffness, and lameness.

> **Note:** A relatively new therapy, extracorporeal shock wave therapy (ESWT) has been reported to have beneficial effects on chronic equine joint problems. See page 65 for more information.
>
>

Spavin

Spavin is a degenerative joint disease of the hock, and it is a common cause of lameness. Spavins may cause obvious leg deformities, as in the case of jack spavin or bone spavin.

An old bone spavin injury will appear as a hard, bony bump on the horse's hock (see illustration). Bone spavin results in a chronic lameness that worsens with exercise. Because bone spavin affects the lower hock, where there is not a lot of joint motion, the hock joints may eventually fuse and stabilize. In such cases, the horse may regain some measure of soundness.

Blind spavin is a hock joint inflammation that resides between the bones and will eventually deteriorate into bone spavin. Bone damage is present in blind spavin, but no obvious bony enlargement can be observed on the horse's leg. Blind spavin may begin as lameness or joint stiffness that improves temporarily as a horse warms up and reappears after the horse cools down.

Bog spavin results in an obvious, fluid-filled swelling of the joint capsule, generally found in front of the hock (see illustration). Bog spavin affects the upper hock joint. Acute bog spavin starts out with sudden swelling of the joint, accompanied by varying degrees of lameness. Bog spavin swelling may become permanent. Depending

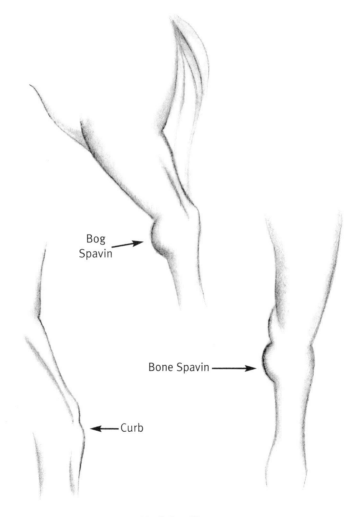

Bog Spavin

Bone Spavin

Curb

Hock Swellings

on the severity of the original injury, the swelling may be chronic, but it will not necessarily be accompanied by lameness.

Treatment: Treatments for acute spavin injuries include bandaging, cold therapy, pain and inflammation medications, and rest. X-ray analysis by your veterinarian will give an idea of the extent of the damage. Your vet may also recommend injections of hyaluronic acid and steroids to help reduce inflammation. Oral supplements such as glucosamine or MSM have been reported to be beneficial.

Sesamoiditis

When the fetlock is sprained, damage to the three distal ligaments can lead to problems in the fetlock joint. There may be heat and swelling in the fetlock area and lameness. Severe ligament damage leads to a degenerative joint disease known as sesamoiditis. Early sesamoiditis may not cause lameness, but the fetlock area will be tender when probed, and the fetlock joint will be somewhat stiff. Inflammation, swelling, and lameness vary with the extent of the injury.

Treatment: If sesamoiditis is suspected, the horse should be confined to his stall and a vet should be contacted immediately. The joint can become inflamed and may even fracture if the condition is neglected. Treatment may include x-rays, several months of stall rest, and anti-inflammatories.

Ringbone

Ringbone is a name given to an unsoundness of the pastern and coffin area. Ringbone is a form of arthritis and is characterized by new bone growth. This new bone growth leaves an obvious swelling around the coronary band, known as low ringbone (see illustration), or circling the area midway between the coronary band and fetlock, known as high ringbone. Ringbone results from repeated tendon and ligament injuries. Symptoms of ringbone include heat, swelling, and lameness.

Treatment: Treatment of acute ringbone starts with x-rays. The joint may have to be immobilized with a cast for several weeks. Treatment may also include oral anti-inflammatory medications, steroid

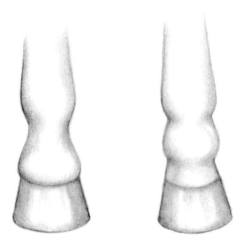

High and Low Ringbone

injections, and several more months of rest. In advanced cases, where a lot of new bone growth has occurred, surgical fusion of the joints may be the only option.

Note: Extracorporeal shock wave therapy has been reported to have beneficial results when used to treat ringbone (see page 65 for more information.)

Cannon Injuries

Bucked Shins

Bucked shins are caused by unusual stress to the cannon bone. Strenuous activities, such as pounding down a racetrack, are extremely stressful to the cannon bones, so such injuries are commonly found among young racehorses. The membrane covering the bone can rupture, and if the horse is not rested and allowed to recover, stress fractures may also result. Recent bucked shin injuries will appear as hot, painful swellings over the front part of the cannon bone, and will result in lameness. Old, healed bucked shins will appear as a cold, permanent lump on the front of the cannon bone. Unless the original damage was unusually severe, these old, calcified growths shouldn't cause problems.

Treatment: Recent injuries with inflammation, swelling, and lameness should be examined by a vet. The horse should be rested. Cold therapy and support bandages will also help with healing. Your vet may also prescribe bute for the inflammation, and cortisone injections.

Splints

Splints appear as raised, hard knots on the horse's front legs (see illustration below). They are generally found on the inside surface of

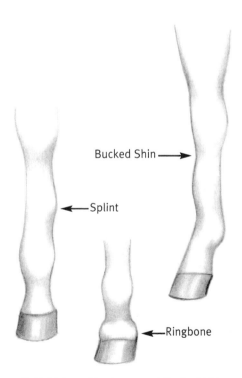

Splint Injury, Ringbone, and Bucked Shin

the front legs, about midway down. The splint bones are connected to, and run parallel to, the cannon bones. They are remainders of prehistoric toes, and serve no real purpose.

One type of splint is caused when the ligament connecting the splint bone to the cannon bone is torn. Another type of injury, often mistaken for splints, is caused by a direct hit to the cannon bone. Inflammation of the membrane protecting the cannon bone can also result in inflammation, calcification, and a permanent lump.

Treatment: In the case of a freshly popped splint, confine the horse to his stall, and call the vet. A vet should examine the horse to make sure there is no other damage to ligaments, tendons, and bones in addition to the splint injury. Ask the vet about giving the horse anti-inflammatory medications.

Bursitis

The bursa act as fluid-filled cushioning and lubricating systems between the joints and tendons of a horse. When a bursa is injured,

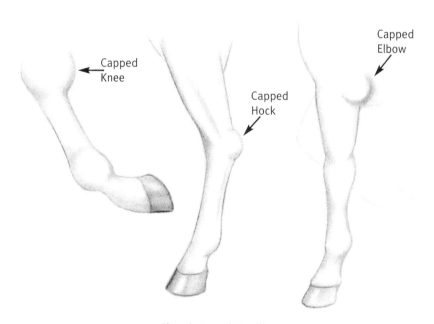

Chronic Bursal Swellings

painful swelling and inflammation can result in lameness. This is the case with cunnean tendon bursitis (jacks). Jacks is a common problem with standardbred racehorses, and it generally causes lameness in both back legs. This lameness may be treated with rest, anti-inflammatory medications, hyaluronic acid injections, and corrective shoeing. If more conservative treatments don't work, surgery is an option.

When bursa are constantly reinjured, the tissue becomes thickened and scarred, and the swelling becomes chronic. Capped elbow, capped hock, and capped knee (see illustration) are chronic bursal swellings that are generally regarded as cosmetic problems, unless abscesses develop. These bursal swellings start out as soft, fluid-filled masses, warm with inflammation. Old bursal swellings are cold, hard, and fibrous to the touch.

Treatment: A veterinarian can drain the swollen bursa and inject corticosteroids or iodine. Recent injuries can benefit from cold therapy, such as ice packing and hosing the affected area with cold water. Pressure bandages are also a recommended part of the treatment.

Hoof Problems

Inspecting the coronet area.

The coronet area (the area immediately above the hoof) should feel cool to the touch, as should the hoof wall below it. There should be no evidence of swelling. Sores, injuries, or any irregularities in the coronet area are a great cause for concern, as damage to the coronet affects the proper growth of the hoof wall.

Quittor is the result of an abscess infection that has spread to the cartilage or an infected wound. Running sores in the coronet area are evidence of severe infection. Call your vet. The wound will have to be cleaned and drained. The owner will also have to keep the wound clean and bandaged after veterinary treatment. The vet may prescribe pain relievers and a tetanus shot if the horse needs one, as well as antibiotics.

Removing loose shoes.

A horse rescued from bad circumstances may be poorly shod and in need of hoof trimming. Loose shoes should be removed, preferably by a farrier. If they are loose enough to create a hazard, you can try to remove them yourself, but if this is not done carefully, the hoof wall can be damaged. First, you will have to file off the bent-over nails on the outside of the hoof (known as clinches), or open them so that the nails can slide back through the hoof wall. Don't try to remove the shoe without opening or cutting off the clinches, or you will damage the horse's hooves.

After opening the clinches, you can remove the individual nails. If you can't remove the individual nails, you may have to loosen the shoe at the heel first. Starting at the outside edge, pry the shoe away from the hoof wall. When you are pulling off the shoe, pull toward the frog, not toward the outside of the hoof. If you find that the hoof is badly damaged after removing the shoe, the hoof edges can be wrapped with duct tape or bandages, or a boot can be used to protect the hoof. Otherwise, the horse should be confined to his stall until you can locate a professional farrier.

Inspecting the Hoof Wall

The surface of the hoof should be fairly smooth and slightly convex when viewed from the side. If the hoof profile is obviously dished, there may be a problem. The hoof wall should meet the ground evenly. If the hooves sweep off to one side, flare out at the bottom, or appear ragged around the edges, or the toes appear overly long in proportion to the rest of the hoof (see photo below), the horse will need a farrier's attention. Ignoring hoof problems can lead to serious injuries.

Check the hoof walls for holes, suspicious-looking bulges, and cracks. Vertical cracks that start from the ground, known as grass cracks, can be caused from letting a horse's hooves grow too long in the toe (see photo below) or from exposing the hoof to too much moisture. Hoof sealers can help protect the hoof from moisture. Vitamin deficiencies can also cause cracks. Biotin supplements can be added to a horse's feed to help harden the hooves.

Types of hoof cracks

Vertical cracks that start from the coronet band, known as sand cracks, are caused by gravel or by blows to the hoof, as are horizontal cracks. As a general rule, horizontal cracks are not as serious as vertical cracks because they are less likely to expand and cause problems like lameness.

Horizontal cracks, known as blow-outs, may be the result of a blow to the hoof, or an abscess may be under the hoof wall. Though horizontal cracks do not generally cause lameness, they should be brought to the attention of a farrier since they may be evidence of infection beneath the hoof wall that will have to be treated.

Though shallow surface cracks can be stabilized by rasping a bit of the hoof off at right angles to the leading edge of the crack, deeper cracks, especially if they are in the coronet area, require the attention of a vet or professional farrier. If heat, lameness, blood, or pus is present, the hoof needs to be thoroughly cleaned and protected by bandaging or by applying a commercial boot. The horse should be kept in a clean, deeply bedded stall until a veterinarian can examine the injury.

Checking for Sole Injuries

To inspect the bottom of a horse's hoof, use a hoof pick to thoroughly clean the area so that any injuries can be seen. The hoof wall should be neatly trimmed and even with the surface of the frog of the foot. Both sides of the hoof wall should be of equal length. The sole of the foot should be slightly dished inward. Flat-footed horses are prone to injury.

Observe the color of the sole of the horse's hoof. Reddish-brown areas, especially in the presence of lameness, are evidence of sole bruises. The reddish-brown color is due to blood collecting beneath the surface. Sole bruises may be healed with rest alone unless an abscess forms.

Abscesses

Abscesses are pockets of infection that will cause a horse to turn up severely lame. If left untreated, sole abscesses can infect and destroy all the important structures of the foot.

Not all foot injuries are obvious to the naked eye. Sore spots can often be revealed by tapping a hammer on the sole of the foot or by using a hoof tester. Puncture wounds can close back over and may be invisible, unless the offending object is still lodged in the horse's foot. Talk to a vet before attempting to remove a nail or other sharp object from a deep puncture wound. Deep puncture wounds require veterinary attention. Untreated puncture wounds can result in inflammation and infection spreading to other systems of the foot. The horse may need a tetanus shot. The wound will have to be opened in order to facilitate cleaning and irrigation of the damaged area with an antiseptic solution, such as Betadine, and to allow for drainage. The wound will need to be cleaned daily, and the horse confined to a clean stall.

Treatment: Abscesses generally require veterinary treatment, including tetanus shots. Part of the horn over the bruise may have to be removed and the abscess enlarged so that it can be flushed out. After treating the horse's foot, the vet will wrap it for you the first time. Pay attention to how he does this. The foot will need to be continually bandaged to prevent contamination for the first few weeks, especially if the abscess is located in the sole of the foot. The abscess will also need to be periodically soaked with Epsom salts and flushed out with a plastic syringe containing Epsom salt solution. The horse will have to be confined to a clean, dry stall, until the abscess has started to heal.

Abscesses located on the sole of the foot will require some kind of foot protection. If the horse gives you a lot of trouble over wrapping his feet, HOOFix boots, manufactured by Plum Shade Farm in Coateville, Pennsylvania, (610–486–0708) work well. Hoofix boots are soft, durable, flexible cloth padded boots, and can be slipped on and off a horse's foot fairly quickly and easily. They also have Velcro closures, which are quick and easy to fasten. You can purchase the whole HOOFix kit and use them as soaking boots. The kit includes a plastic liner, Epsom salts, bandages, and a syringe, as well as the boots.

HOOFix boots can be left on a horse's feet twenty-four hours per day, if necessary. Limited turnout is possible, though having used these boots, I recommend the horse be confined to a round pen or very small paddock with good, level footing in dry conditions, if he is left unsupervised. These boots are also useful to take on trail rides as emergency hoof protection. But they should only be used to prevent further injury to the hoof since they were not designed as a riding boot.

The boots are already padded on the bottom, but the padding can be easily supplemented with a small disposable diaper, impregnated with an Epsom salt poultice, icthammol drawing salve, or any other medication recommended by your veterinarian.

Laminitis

Sore spots on the sole of a horse's foot can be a symptom of much more than a simple bruise. Pain in the toe area of the sole may be a symptom of laminitis, also called founder. Acute laminitis is a medical emergency. The horse will adopt a peculiar stance, trying to shift his weight off the front feet and onto the back feet (see illustration that follows). During especially severe attacks, the horse will lie down, and may moan and groan with pain. During an acute attack, the digital pulse can be very strong in the fetlock.

In the old days, horsemen used to stand a foundering horse in an icy stream. Later, it was decided that lack of circulation caused founder damage, so cold therapy fell out of favor. Recent research indicates that inflammation causes most founder damage, and therefore the old timers had it right to begin with. So packing your horse's feet with ice or cooling the inflammation with water until the vet arrives is a good idea. You can also ask your vet about administering an anti-inflammatory medication, such as Banamine.

Laminitis stance

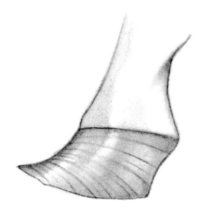

Hoof distortion known as "slipper foot," resulting from severe, chronic laminitis. Prominent, wavy ridges can be seen on the surface of the hoof. Note that these ridges are wider at the heel than at the toe. The toe is curled up and the hoof profile is dished.

Chronic laminitis due to disease or severe neglect can cause some obvious hoof distortions. The profile of the hoof may appear dished when viewed from the side. The surface of the hoof wall may look like something that washed up on a beach at low tide. Stress from disease or neglect may cause stress ridges on the hoof surface. Laminitis ridges have a peculiar shape, due to the fact that the heel is growing faster than the toe. The ridges will be prominent and deep, and will be wider at the heel than at the toe. The hoof wall may be unusually wide and distorted when viewed from the bottom surface.

More information on laminitis is available in chapter three, "Caring for Equine Senior Citizens," beginning on page 91.

White Line Disease

White line disease is a bacterial or fungal disease of the white line area of the hoof. The white line is found just inside of and bordering the hoof wall, on the sole of the horse's foot (see illustration below). Once it has invaded the area behind the hoof wall, white line disease destroys the hoof material, leaving a blackened, mealy material in its wake. The infection can spread all the way from the sole of the foot up to the coronary band. Depending on the extent of the damage,

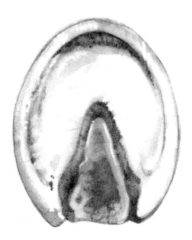

Hoof separation as a result of white line disease.

white line disease will need to be treated by a vet or professional farrier. The diseased areas of the hoof must be removed and the hoof packed with medicated dressings. Special shoeing techniques, including pads and partial reconstruction of the hoof with synthetic materials, may also be necessary.

Thrush

The frog of the foot should be a clean, hard, tough, rubbery structure (see photo below). The triangular cleft of the frog should be clean and open. If the cleft is a swollen, nasty-smelling crack, and is filled with black, tarry material, the horse is probably suffering from thrush. Thrush is a bacterial infection caused from filth and wetness. It thrives in hooves packed with dirt and where oxygen can't reach. The foot should be cleaned thoroughly, and the dead, ragged parts of the frog removed. Commercial products are available for treating thrush and can be obtained from your vet or a supply house.

Navicular Disease

Pain over the central third of the frog can be an indication of a degenerative condition of the navicular complex known as navicular disease. The navicular complex includes the navicular bone, deep digital flexor tendon, coffin joint, and supporting ligaments. Most of the pain from navicular disease is concentrated in the heel, beneath the central area of the frog, because the source of the pain—the navicular bone and bursa—are located in that area. Navicular disease results in a chronic lameness of the front feet.

Treatments: Treatment of navicular disease will require the help of a veterinarian and a capable farrier who is familiar with therapeutic shoeing methods. Veterinary treatment generally includes anti-inflammatory medications. Vets may also recommend the use of isoxsuprine hydrochloride to improve blood circulation to the navicular bone. Navicular disease has reportedly shown improvement after being treated with extracorporeal shock wave therapy.

When noninvasive methods do not work, a common surgical procedure known as palmar digital neurectomy—removing the digital nerves of the foot—may relieve navicular pain and allow the horse to be usable again. Possible complications of such surgery should be discussed with your vet.

References and Sources of Additional Information

Adams, Stephen B., DVM, MS, DACVS. "Shockwave Therapy for Horses," June 3, 2002, www.vet.purdue.edu/horses/shockwavelay mandescrip.htm (accessed September 14, 2004).

Allen, Janice B., PhD, Brian C. Gilger, DVM, MS, David A. Wilkie, DVM, Michael G. Davidson, MS. "Use of an intravitreal sustained-release cyclosporine delivery device for treatment of equine recurrent uveitis," *Abstract-American Journal of Veterinary Research*, December 2001, Vol. 62, No. 12, Pages 1892–1896.

Equine Research, *Lameness: Recognizing and Treating the Horse's Most Common Ailment*, Lyons Press, 2005.

Giffen, James, MD, and Tom Gore, DVM. *Horse Owner's Veterinary Handbook*, 2nd Edition, Howell Book House, 1989.

Kaneps, Andris J., DVM, PhD. "Equine Tendon Injuries and Treatment," Ohio State University, Gallopers Australia Wide Bloodstock Website: gallopers. com.

Macallister, Carolynn. F-9120, "Respiratory Diseases in Horses: What You Can Do to Prevent Them," Oklahoma Cooperative Extension Service, December 3, 2004, www.osuextra.com (accessed September 14, 2004).

McIllwraith, Wayne C., BVSc, PhD. "Traumatic Joint Injuries and Disease," Colorado State University Orthaepaedic Research Center Website, http://equineortho.colostate.edu/faq (January 31, 2005).

McClure, Scott. "New Treatment for Musculoskeletal Diseases Available at Purdue," Vol. 2, Issue No. 1, 1999, www.vet.purdue.edu/horses/MusculoskeletalDisease.html.

Nebraska Cooperative Extension G00–1403-A, "Basics of Feeding Horses: Reading the Feed Tag," *Nebguide*, http://ianrpubs.unl.edu/horse/g1403.htm (accessed March 6, 2004).

Ramey, David W., DVM. *Medications and Supplements for the Horse*, Howell Book House, 1996.

Schwab, R. Paul, DVM. "Doctor's Corner: Common Problems of the Equine Eye," *The Northwest Horse Source*, October 2003, www.nwhorsesource.com.

Caring for Equine Senior Citizens

According to the *Guinness Book of World Records*, a horse by the name of Old Billy lived until the incredible age of sixty-two. Billy died in 1822, and still holds the record for equine longevity. Old Billy made the record books back then, and his sixty-two-year life span is still considered amazing, even in modern times. Although recent advances in veterinary and animal husbandry techniques have greatly increased the possibility that a horse will stay sound past the age of twenty, it still takes a bit of luck for a horse to make it past thirty.

Horses in Billy's time were employed in transportation and farming, and with few exceptions they were generally regarded with the same practical sentimentality reserved for cars or tractors. The lives of horses usually ended when their usefulness ended. Nowadays, horses are mainly valued as companion animals. Although some owners regard equines as hairy motorcycles, to be discarded as soon as mechanical problems become inconvenient, others develop strong emotional ties, and their elderly horses become like members of the family.

This chapter is dedicated to those horse owners who are willing to spend the time and money required to keep an old pensioner comfortable, even when he is little more than a pasture ornament, and the most exercise he ever gets is walking to the barn to be fed. If owners of elderly equines provide good care and remain alert to changes in physical condition and behavior, horses can remain healthy well into their late twenties.

Your horse may be over the hill, but you can still enjoy the view from his back. He may not win the Kentucky Derby, but he's probably sound enough for many horseback activities. You may already be at an age to enjoy a good old pony you can take short naps on, as opposed to a fireball that can outrun whitetail deer on the trails.

Older horses have definite advantages, especially on trail rides. Equine senior citizens tend to have fewer temper tantrums over control issues. They are less likely to pitch a fit at the sound of a car with a loud boom box, or try to convince you that great white sharks live in the shallow creek you are attempting to cross. Senior horses have been there, done that, and no longer worry about imaginary dangers. Older horses also tend to have more patience with inexperienced riders and children. If your old pensioner can manage a few trips around the pasture, he may still be useful as an occasional guest horse or babysitter.

Many older horses can have useful second careers. A senior show horse with years of experience under his girth may be a better choice for younger horse show competitors and adult beginners. Older horses are also valuable assets to handicapped riding programs. Unless you are trying to outrun a bear, older horses are better in emergency situations, when a calm, gentle disposition is vital. The following story demonstrates this point.

The Endurance Ride

Standing about 13.5 hands, Belle is a pretty little mustang mare, though not very impressive to look at. A gentle creature, she never really gets excited about anything. Jackie, Belle's owner, is a warm, attractive person, whose dark hair and high cheekbones reveal Cherokee ancestry. Jackie leads Belle around the yard frequently with a cargo of grandchildren. Belle is also a good riding horse for adults, a totally bombproof trail mount.

Despite the Bureau of Land Management brand she wears on her neck, it is hard to believe that Belle once ran wild on the western plains. She may have been adopted for $125 more than twenty years ago, but Jackie probably wouldn't take a million dollars for her now. Belle proved her true worth during one of the worst trials of Jackie's life.

It all started when Jackie's husband, Joe, took their ATV out for a spin in the nearby woods. There were lots of trails to explore, and friends nearby to visit, so Jackie did not get really concerned about his absence until the sun was starting to set, and a gathering storm was making the sky even darker.

Jackie made some phone calls but did not locate Joe. She saddled up Belle and searched the woods for him; still no luck. Panic started to set in. She made a call to 911, and searchers arrived to comb the woods. Jackie and Belle were out there too, riding through a thunderstorm, in the dark, amid flashing searchlights and rescue workers on ATVs. They crossed swollen streams and searched down narrow, rough trails through the tangled woods. Belle carried Jackie quietly and safely through it all.

The searchers could find no sign of Joe in the storm-tossed woods. "He's probably holed up, out of the rain somewhere in a barn, or visiting with a friend," the searchers tried to reassure Jackie. But she knew better.

Jackie could not bear the thought of Joe lying unconscious out there somewhere in the dark acres of wilderness, or wandering hurt, lost, and confused in the cold rain. She did not sleep during what remained of a night of pure hell.

Before first light, Jackie saddled Belle and headed back into the woods to find her husband. She did not get far before she heard an answer to her frantic calls. Though Joe had not been far from home, rescue teams missed him completely in the dense underbrush. Joe had been unconscious and unable to call for help for most of the night.

Joe could not walk out of the woods due to extensive injuries. Somehow, Jackie managed to lift him onto Belle's back. The little horse stood quietly while Jackie got on behind her husband. Jackie held Joe in the saddle, riding double. Belle carried them home safely, and Joe was taken by ambulance to the hospital.

Joe is now out of the hospital and recovering from his injuries at home. Jackie takes extra good care of him, and she makes sure a certain little mustang horse standing out in the pasture gets some special care as well.

General Considerations

Exercise and Elderly Horses

Belle, the mustang in the above story, was still in good health and perfectly sound, despite her advancing years. This is not unusual. Even mustangs in the wild can live more than twenty years if the environment is healthy, with good forage and plenty of water. Wild horses get plenty of exercise. They travel great distances in search of food and water.

Domestic horses need regular exercise as well. Being kept in a stall twenty-four hours a day is not healthy for any horse. Turnout time and riding are beneficial, unless an elderly horse has a severe medical condition requiring stall confinement. Owners of elderly equines need to be alert to changes in behavior and use common sense regarding how much exercise a horse should get. Listen to what he tells you under saddle. A horse that is reluctant to move, especially one that has been cooperative in the past, shortens his stride, and lays his ears back when asked to go faster than a walk could be in pain from arthritis or some other complaint. Medical problems must be addressed to keep your horse as comfortable as possible.

Arthritis and Exercise

Arthritis is a painful, chronic inflammation of the joints caused by injury or disease. As a horse ages, the fluid protecting his joints grows thin. Cartilage starts to wear out and tendons and ligaments stretch. Hard new bone begins to replace the soft cartilage that once cushioned the joint, forming painful spurs.

If your horse displays symptoms of arthritis, such as swelling, inflammation, stiffness, or lameness, call your veterinarian. Treatments are available. Hyaluronic acid injections stimulate the production of joint fluid, improve joint lubrication, and have anti-inflammatory benefits. Anti-inflammatory drugs, such as phenylbutazone or "bute," help to relieve pain. Over-the-counter medications, such as chondroitin sulfate and MSM, can be mixed with the horse's feed, and have been reported to increase flexibility. A good farrier should be able to offer shoeing and hoof trimming techniques that will help keep your horse comfortable.

If you own a reasonably sound equine senior citizen, regular exercise such as leisurely trail rides will help keep him that way. Mild stiffness that soon disappears after a gentle warm-up is not much cause for concern. But exercising a horse in obvious pain, whose joints are inflamed, can cause serious damage, so talk to your vet before starting an exercise program.

Gentle riding at a walk, and trotting for short distances, will help preserve muscle mass and keep joints flexible. Two or three rides a week should be sufficient. A horse that is too frail to ride can be hand-walked with a lead rope. At the very least, he should be allowed access to a paddock and turned out regularly.

Exhaustion and Overheating

Use common sense. How much exercise your horse is able to tolerate also depends on what he's used to. Say you gently ride your horse about once a week, for half an hour, in a flat pasture, as a normal routine. You spend most of that time at a walk, occasionally breaking into a trot for short periods. Then one day, you take him on a fast two-hour trail ride, trotting and cantering most of the way, in rugged country. Exercising an old horse more strenuously than usual is asking for trouble. A young horse could overheat and colic under those circumstances.

Slow down and let your horse travel at the pace that is comfortable for him (unless he's an ex-racehorse who likes to run). It is best to travel at a walk most of the time, trotting occasionally for short distances. If he wants to canter going uphill, let him. Cantering uphill is easier on his joints and tendons; but make sure you give him a breather at the top of steep hills. Avoid deep mud holes. Old tendons don't need the added stress. Struggling through deep mud can injure a horse's stifles.

If your horse starts behaving sluggishly on the trail, stumbles a lot, and falls behind the other horses, it may be a sign that he's becoming overly fatigued. Another sign of extreme fatigue may be that he's still breathing hard while traveling on level ground. You've overdone it, and the consequences could be serious. Get off his back, loosen the cinch, and let him rest.

If a horse overheats, his legs may be hosed down with cool water to reduce his body temperature. Pay special attention to the insides of the legs. Large arteries are located there, and water applied to those areas will help cool him down faster. If you're in the wilderness, take him to the nearest creek and use water to cool his head, chest, shoulders, and legs. Let him drink, but not too much at a time, as he could founder. If he doesn't want to move, don't force him. Massage the leg muscles and let him stand for a while. When he's ready to move, hand-walk him until he cools off. If the horse stands with his head hanging, sides heaving, and shows no interest in grass or water, get help. Severe cases of overheating require emergency treatment by a veterinarian.

During the summer months, senior horses also have more trouble regulating their body temperature. If your horse has a long coat, you can clip it short to keep him comfortable. It may not be advisable to ride him at all on extremely hot or cold days.

Extreme Weather

Senior horses need to be protected from summer and winter temperature extremes. Despite their reputation, horses do not always have enough sense to get in out of a freezing rain, snow, or winter wind. I have observed horses standing outside, totally ignoring an open barn door for hours with snow accumulating on their backs and icicles hanging off their belly hair. Winter wind and freezing rain can chill a horse's body, despite the fact that Mother Nature has provided these animals with a hair coat that traps heat and a digestive system that burns hay like a small furnace. Cold winter wind can allow trapped heat in the coat to escape. Freezing rain can also sabotage Mother Nature's efforts to keep the horse warm. If you live in a part of the country where the weather can change radically in the early spring and fall, be especially cautious.

Make sure your elderly horse has adequate shelter. He should have protection from the cold and access to shade on hot days. A run-in shelter, preferably a solid structure, with a roof and at least three sides should be provided. Shelter should be appropriate for the weather conditions of the region in which the animal is located.

If you see your elderly horse shivering in cold weather, blanket him. If you turn him out with a blanket, make sure it is a turnout

Got carrots? Equine Seniors need shelter during cold weather.

blanket designed for that purpose and made with a fabric that repels moisture. Horse hair naturally traps heat provided the coat is clean enough to be fluffy, but a thin, inadequate turnout blanket can make things worse by flattening down the hair coat.

Grumpy Old Geldings

Careful attention should be paid to changes in behavior. A reluctant or hostile attitude when being handled can signal a health problem. A horse that won't lift a leg for the farrier could be having trouble balancing on three legs. Balance problems could be due to injury, arthritis, or foot problems. Allow frequent rest periods with all four feet planted on the ground during farrier visits. A horse that doesn't want to be bridled or tosses his head and fights the bit could be experiencing pain from dental problems, and he may need to have his teeth floated by a vet or equine dentist.

If an elderly horse shies at objects previously ignored, he may not be seeing things as clearly these days. An old horse's retinas may thicken over the years, causing vision to deteriorate. You may notice a slight blue cast to your elderly horse's eye; this is normal. However, a milky cast may indicate the development of cataracts and is cause for concern. Bumping into things and stumbling over slight changes in terrain may also indicate vision problems. Medical causes should always be considered when there are any abrupt changes in a horse's behavior.

If your pensioner is out in the pasture with a herd of younger horses, pay attention to what's going on out there. He may not be able to maintain his previous position in the pecking order, and the younger horses may start to bully him and make his life miserable. If you feed horses out in the pasture, more aggressive herd members may prevent him from eating. The older horse might start bolting his food to keep others from taking it away from him, increasing the dangers of choke or colic. It may be necessary to feed the older horse separately to ensure that he gets an equal share. At the very least, one or two more piles of hay than the number of horses being fed in the pasture should be provided, and the piles should be spaced farther apart.

Herd harassment can also keep the senior horse from getting adequate rest, and cause serious injuries. Troublemakers should be housed elsewhere, but complete removal of other horses is not advisable. Horses are herd animals and may become neurotic as a result of total isolation. Even if he is kept in a separate paddock, the older horse should have company nearby.

Common Senior Horse Health Problems

Coat and Skin

An elderly horse that maintains an unusually long, thick, coarse hair coat well into summer, may be developing Cushing's disease. An unusually long coat may also be a sign that an older horse is having trouble maintaining his body temperature due to illness, or he may be suffering from nutritional deficiencies caused by age-related systemic problems.

Check the skin surface carefully. The immune systems of elderly horses may weaken with age, making them susceptible to bacterial and fungus infections. Pimple-like bumps on the skin, crusty patches, excessive dander, and patchy hair loss are all signs of skin problems.

Hoof Problems

Hooves become more brittle with age and tend to crack. One factor that aggravates the problem is excess moisture. Hooves expand with moisture, then dry out and contract. Oils leach out during this process and cracks can develop. If you wash and dry your hands several times in the course of a day, you can observe the same effect on your own skin and nails. Horses should not be allowed to stand constantly in muddy areas, especially where there is standing water. Dry living quarters are important. Hoof sealant can be used to help repel moisture, but consult your veterinarian before using any hoof-care product. Diaper rash medication, massaged into a horse's coronet band, will help stimulate circulation in that area and may relieve some of the dryness. Icthammol dressing can be used as a very mild hoof dressing, and it can also be applied to skin conditions as well. Over-the-counter biotin supplements may be added to the horse's feed to help strengthen the hoof walls.

If you are not riding your elderly horse very much, you may elect to keep him barefoot, but don't neglect his hooves. Regular trimming by a good farrier is even more important as horses age. Long hooves will develop cracks and should be trimmed every six weeks.

Respiratory Problems

Elderly horses have weakened immune systems and are more susceptible to colds and respiratory infections. If your horse is running a fever of more than 101 degrees Fahrenheit, his nose is running, and the discharge is milky, call your veterinarian.

Frequent coughing that worsens during exercise and nasal discharge that persists over a long period of time, especially in dusty areas, may be signs that a horse is developing chronic obstructive pulmonary disease, or heaves. Horses with severe heaves will eventually develop a "heave line" at the base of their ribs. It appears as a long indentation, as though a line was drawn there with the tip of your finger, and is especially obvious during labored breathing. Horses with severe heaves will display labored breathing even at rest. Horses with heaves also tend to have problems maintaining their weight and condition.

Colic

Elderly horses may be more prone to colic as a result of dental problems and digestive inefficiency related to age. An old horse who refuses to eat or drink is a cause for immediate concern, especially if he shows signs of pain—sweating, wringing his tail, or kicking at his stomach. He will have an anxious expression. You will notice his stomach muscles cramping, and his sides may appear bloated. Press your ear to his flanks. In a healthy horse, you should hear stomach noises that will sound somewhat like dishwater going down the drain. Check both sides. Dead silence is a sign of impaction colic. Impaction colic is caused by a blockage in the intestines. In the worst-case scenario, the intestines may actually be twisted shut. In the case of the gaseous variety of colic, stomach noises may be exaggerated in the extreme and often will be accompanied by diarrhea.

Pale gum color is an indicator that the horse is in dire straits and may go into shock, as is a pulse elevated to more than sixty beats per minute. A horse with severe colic will also lie down and roll frequently in a vain effort to relieve the pain in his abdomen.

Call the vet immediately. Walk the horse and try to keep him on his feet until the vet arrives. Walking the horse helps to pass the gas that accompanies an attack of colic. Consult your veterinarian before taking any other action. A dose of Banamine (flunixin meglumine) can help ease the pain. In the case of impaction colic, a dose of mineral oil can also be beneficial. Mineral oil will coat a horse's stomach and intestines, and it may help reduce the absorption of toxins. If the horse has gaseous diarrhea, ask your vet about giving the horse some Peptol Bismol. Be sure to inform the veterinarian of any medications the horse receives. More information on colic is available in chapter two, "Caring for Rescue Horses," page 44.

Dental Problems

Senior horses often develop sharp points on their teeth, which cause painful sores and cuts in their mouths. When being ridden, a horse experiencing pain from dental problems will chew at the bit, gape his mouth, and toss his head. While eating, feed may dribble from the corners of the horse's mouth, and he may tilt his head to the side while chewing. Some horses can be observed splashing and mouthing the water in buckets, as though trying to relieve pain by wetting their mouths. They may also try to dip a mouthful of feed in water to soften it. A horse with a sore mouth may refuse to eat his grain, preferring his hay instead. If a horse's teeth are in really bad shape, he may stop eating altogether. A dose of Banamine or bute will help relieve pain temporarily, but the horse's teeth will need professional attention as soon as possible.

Most large animal veterinarians can float a horse's teeth (filing the sharp points down), but in some rare cases, where special grinding tools are required that your vet doesn't normally keep on hand, it may be necessary to retain the services of an equine dentist. If you do use an equine dentist, make sure he has good references.

Some dental procedures require strong tranquilizers to immobilize the horse. Dental surgery, removing wolf teeth, or trimming a horse's canines are procedures best performed under veterinary supervision, even if you do employ an equine dentist. If you have any doubts at all about your horse's willingness to cooperate, it is best to have a veterinarian there to administer a tranquilizer. Otherwise, the dentist will accomplish very little while struggling with a 1,200-pound horse who does not appreciate a trip to the dentist any more than you do. Whichever professional you choose, aged horses should have their teeth checked at least once a year; twice yearly is best.

Choking Due to Dental Problems

Dental problems increase the danger of choking. A horse can choke on grain or other food when it is inadequately chewed, causing an impaction in the esophagus. A choking horse will refuse to eat. He will stretch his neck and cough. A heavy nasal discharge will run from his nose. You will see feed particles in the discharge from his nose and mouth. You may be able to feel a hard lump under his throatlatch where the impaction is located.

Unlike in humans, when a horse's esophagus is blocked by food or other obstruction there isn't immediate danger of suffocation. Don't panic. But choking is still a health emergency requiring prompt veterinary care as soon as possible. A veterinarian may give the horse medication to relax the esophagus, or he may insert a nasal tube and flush out the obstruction with warm water. The horse should also be thoroughly examined after an episode of choke, to ensure that there is no permanent damage or chronic stricture (narrowing of the esophagus). Inflammation or stricture may require that the horse be put on soft, moist food until the problem is corrected.

Feeding Senior Horses

An old horse's back teeth may get worn down to the point of being useless, or he may lose them altogether. If a horse can't chew feed thoroughly, he is more likely to choke, or the incompletely chewed mass could become impacted in the intestines, causing colic. A horse with dental problems may also lose weight, as inadequately chewed food is not digested efficiently.

The owner of a horse who is physically unable to chew his food efficiently can buy commercial feeds, such as Equine Senior or Nutrena Senior, specifically designed for elderly equines. Senior pelleted feeds dissolve easily and can be softened with water to the consistency of soup if necessary, and they are specially processed to be easily digestible. Though they are often advertised as complete feeds, you should provide hay or some other form of roughage if at all possible.

Cut up hay to make it easier to chew or purchase a mechanical shredder. Hay purchased for an old horse, or any horse for that matter, should be leafy in texture and not have a lot of tough stems. Timothy, orchard grass, and brome grass are some of the more easily chewed varieties of hay.

Hay Substitutes

Alfalfa cubes can be soaked in warm water and fed to the horse wet. Some horses don't care for wet food. However, sliced carrots or other treats can be added to the wet alfalfa to tempt them to try it. Alfalfa should not be fed to horses with certain health problems, such as kidney or liver dysfunction, as their systems cannot handle the protein and calcium content. Dry alfalfa cubes present a choking hazard to horses with dental problems and horses that bolt their food.

Beet pulp can also be soaked with water and used as a hay substitute. Beet pulp is a great source of nutrition, contains about 10 percent protein, and is easy to digest. Dry beet pulp can cause a horse to choke if he has dental problems or tends to bolt down his food. If you have your feed custom-mixed at the mill, you can have dry beet pulp ground into your regular mix. Horses seem to eat it better when it is mixed in with their regular feed. Beet pulp is also available in pellets, although pellets will not provide the bulk necessary to keep a horse's intestines functioning properly. Some hay will still need to be fed.

Maintaining Weight and Condition

As horses age, they may have problems absorbing nutrients, requiring a diet that is higher in protein and fat to keep a healthy weight. Extruded feeds, which are processed under pressure, are easier for an older horse's system to process. It is also helpful to spread a horses's daily ration of grain over several smaller feedings, since smaller amounts of grain are easier to digest. Supplements containing yeast cultures and probiotic microorganisims aid in digestion.

Nutrena manufactures a feed called Safe Choice that can help put weight on a horse. If the horse has dental issues, you can soften the feed with water, as the pellets absorb water readily. You can pour warm water over the feed and it will soften up within a few minutes. If you have problems introducing your horse to wet feed, you can hide a few thinly sliced slivers of carrot in it, or add a teaspoon of pancake syrup or sugar to the warm water before you pour it over the feed.

Vegetable oil and can be added to a horse's feed to add fat content. Depending on your horse's size, you can slowly work up to as much as two cups of oil per day. Palatable commercial supplements with high fat content can be purchased for horses that do not care for the taste of vegetable oil in their feed.

Processed feeds with crude fat content of 6 percent or more are acceptable for horses needing to gain weight. Feeds with fat content of 10 to 12 percent are available. Underweight horses should have free-choice access to grass hay. Good pasture also helps maintain good condition.

Older horses also need a bit more protein. Feeds with protein content over 12 percent are available and are appropriate for elderly horses, as long as they are not suffering from liver or kidney problems. Linseed meal adds protein and may also help to soften stools in a horse with constipation problems. Soybean meal is a good protein source, but is not as palatable as linseed. Owners who have horse feed custom mixed at a mill can have soybean oil added to the regular mix, as well as some flavoring to improve the taste. Cottonseed meal, peanut meal, safflower meal, gluten meal, fish meals, and brewer's pellets and grains are also used as protein supplements. Commercial protein supplements containing some of these ingredients can be found at your local feed store. If you cannot find these items locally, they can be direct-ordered from companies such as Valley Vet Supply (800–356–1005), Stateline Tack (800–228–9208), and Dover Saddlery (800–989–1500).

Feeding Senior Horses with Health Problems

As a horse ages, his immune system, digestive system, and other organs may deteriorate. An older horse that is unable to digest his food efficiently requires supplemental fat and proteins. Conversely, other health problems may require the owner to strictly limit the horse's consumption of fats, protein, and carbohydrates. Certain diseases more commonly found in elderly horses require careful dietary management.

Cushing's Disease

Cushing's disease results when a benign tumor causes the pituitary gland to secrete abnormal amounts of hormones. Symptoms of Cushing's may include some or all of the following: excessive thirst, excessive urination, and abnormal hair growth that does not shed out in summer. Conformation peculiarities may be noted as well: a cresty neck, a potbelly, and a swayback coupled with loss of muscle over the topline. The natural depression over a horse's eyes may also fill in with fat. Though these changes may cause concern, the most dreaded symptom of Cushing's is laminitis, a crippling disease that can eventually cost a horse his life

Laminitis, also called founder, is caused by inflammation and reduction of blood flow to the laminae, resulting in severe tissue damage. The laminae attach the coffin bone of a horse's foot to the hoof wall. In severe cases of founder, the tissues are so badly damaged that the coffin bone will actually sink down and penetrate the bottom of the horse's foot.

Drugs such as pergolide and cyproheptadine are used to treat Cushing's disease and must be prescribed by your veterinarian. They are expensive, but the development of laminitis can be held off for quite some time if treatment is started early. The horse's general health and comfort will also be greatly improved.

Horses with Cushing's will eventually suffer from laminitis, although they may have the disease for years without manifesting any symptoms of founder. If you suspect that your horse may be foundering, remove all feed from the area and call your vet immediately. Founder is a medical emergency, but the damage can be limited by prompt veterinary care.

Prevention is the best way to keep your horse from foundering. Sweet feeds should be avoided, as should lush spring pasture. Well-cured grass hays, such as timothy, orchard grass, and brome, are safest. Pasture access, hay, and even water intake may need to be restricted in certain situations. Talk to your veterinarian.

Lush spring pasture can overload any horse's digestive system. Caution should always be exercised when turning a horse out on spring pasture for the first time. Overindulgence can result in a case of colic as well as founder. It is safer to feed the horse a ration of hay or other feed before turning him out, so he will not be overly hungry. Otherwise, he may try to gorge himself on the tender new grass.

In the beginning, until the horse's digestive system has had some time to adjust, grazing on pasture should be limited to half-hour periods and increased very slowly. Healthy horses can be safely pastured for one to two hours the first day out. Cushing's horses known to have foundered in the past should not be allowed to graze at night, when sugar levels in pasture grass are highest.

Reduce carbohydrates. Careful feedings of high-fiber, pelleted complete feeds may be the best choice. Complete feeds with fiber content up 30 percent are available and are basically equivalent to a hay diet. Steamed, extruded feeds are easiest to digest. The bulk of these feeds are processed in the small colon and are less likely to overwhelm the hind-gut area of the digestive system, which could lead to founder. Special senior feeds with low levels of carbohydrates can be purchased especially for horses prone to laminitis. Complete feeds should not be fed alone, even if they do contain a high percentage of roughage. The horse should still be fed hay to satisfy the need to chew; otherwise he may start attacking all the wood surfaces in the vicinity. At least a small amount of hay is also needed in the diet to provide the bulk necessary to keep a horse's digestive system functioning properly.

Grain may have to be eliminated from the diet altogether due to high levels of carbohydrates, which can overload the horse's digestive system and lead to founder. If you feed grain at all, you must introduce it gradually. Daily rations, spread out over several small feedings, are preferable to larger amounts fed once or twice daily. You can put some large, smooth, round rocks in the horse's feed tub to slow down his feed consumption, or spread his feed out in a large, shallow tub. Grain rations can also be mixed 50:50 with chopped grass hay to reduce concentrations.

Sudden changes in diet may cause problems with any horse's digestive system and should be introduced gradually. Feeding on a regular schedule is also important. All horses are lovers of routine and have excellent internal clocks, which start the appropriate digestive juices going at the appointed time. Food is the high point of a horse's day. Irregular feed times can upset the digestive system of a healthy horse, let alone a horse prone to laminitis.

Feeds with a higher fat content will not cause laminitis, but do not give your horse too much of any kind of feed. Obesity is not

> **Note:** Any exercise program should be discussed with your vet. Horses suffering from acute laminitis pain should never be exercised. No horse should be subjected to vigorous exercise immediately after eating; wait at least an hour. Horses prone to laminitis should not be exercised on hard surfaces.
>
>

healthy, particularly for a horse with laminitis. Veterinarians will tell you that the hardest thing about managing horse patients with founder is convincing owners not to overfeed. Extra weight adds to the damage done by founder, not to mention the additional stress on an aged horse's heart, lungs, and tendons. Even though your old horse may not be long for this world, and the temptation to spoil him is overwhelming, he needs your help more than your sympathy. Don't give him that extra scoop of feed. When managing horses prone to laminitis, you may even have to restrict water intake.

Horses prone to laminitis can demonstrate insulin resistance similar to human type-2 diabetics. In human cases, doctors often recommend exercise to lower harmful glucose levels. Gentle exercise after eating may be beneficial. Hand-walk if the horse is too fragile to be ridden. Studies have indicated that as little as one half hour of low intensity exercise daily can help to lower harmful glucose levels.

Concentrate on Feeding

Liver Disease

Diets with high protein content are not appropriate for horses with liver problems. Total protein content of feed (including hay) should be restricted to maintenance levels—around 10 percent or less, if possible. Maintenance-level horse feeds average around 8 to 12 percent protein. Corn grain contains approximately 8 to 10 percent protein. Grass hays, on average, contain around 8 percent crude protein. Alfalfa should be avoided. Alfalfa hay can contain as much as 22 percent protein. Corn or maintenance-sweet feeds with a protein content of 8 to 12 percent, combined with quality grass hay for roughage, are appropriate for a horse with liver problems.

Horses with liver problems also can't handle feeds with a high fat content. Total fat content should be restricted to maintenance levels of around 5 to 6 percent or lower, if possible. Dividing the daily ration into several small feedings per day will make it easier for the horse's system to process the food.

Urinary System Problems

Kidney problems are not common in horses, but a horse that drinks and urinates excessively may be suffering from kidney disease. Painful urination, straining, dribbling urine, and urine stains on the legs are all indications of bladder infections, bladder stones, or urinary tract infections. Cushing's disease will also cause the same symptoms.

Kidney Problems

Horses with kidney failure are unable to process calcium adequately, and may develop bladder stones (calculi). Total phosphorus and calcium content of the horse's feed should be kept low and as close to minimum requirements as possible. Most commercially mixed grains contain anywhere from 0.4 percent to 1 percent calcium and phosphorus. A mature horse only requires around 0.3 percent calcium and 0.2 percent phosphorus content. Always remember that the calcium content of your horse's rations should be equal to or higher than the phosphorus content. The calcium/phosphorus ratio should be maintained at 1 to 2 parts calcium to 1 part phosphorus.

Alfalfa should not be fed to a horse with kidney problems, due to high calcium and protein content. Timothy or other good-quality grass hays are acceptable. Clover, wheat bran, and beet pulp should be avoided. An exception to this rule is that beet pulp and wheat bran are acceptable as additives in a processed complete feed, such as extruded or pelleted feeds.

Good-quality grass hay, combined with corn grain or complete feeds designed for maintenance are recommended. Most maintenance feeds have a crude protein content of 8 to 10 percent. High-protein feeds should be avoided. Water should be available at all times.

Any diet for a horse with liver or kidney disease, laminitis, or other serious health problems should be discussed with your vet.

Bladder Stones

Elderly male horses are most likely to develop bladder stones, which cause symptoms similar to colic. Horses with bladder stones may not want to eat or drink due to discomfort, wring their tails, sweat, and show other signs of pain. Also, they will stretch and strain in an effort to urinate, but produce little more than a trickle of liquid. Call the vet immediately. Bladder stones can be life-threatening and may require surgery to treat. A complete blockage is a health emergency, as fluid will accumulate rapidly and poison the horse's system.

Horses with a medical history of developing bladder stones should not be fed high amounts of calcium, magnesium, or phosphorus. Alfalfa should not be fed due to high calcium levels. Maintenance-level commercial feeds, corn, and grass hay are less likely to contribute to the formation of bladder stones.

Chronic Obstructive
Pulmonary Disease (Heaves)

Heaves is a chronic disease of the respiratory system. Exposure to allergens such as molds, hay, or stable dust causes the airways of a horse's lungs to become irritated, obstructed, and inflamed. Dust and mold should be eliminated from the horse's environment as much as possible. Stable dust appears to cause the worst problem.

The horse's condition can be improved by keeping him out of closed-in barn stalls altogether. Provide an open, attached horse porch or three-sided shelter to protect the horse from bad weather. Run-ins should provide good air circulation and be cleaned regularly, as equine waste fumes can aggravate respiratory problems.

If the horse has to be kept in a stall, bedding can be replaced with stall mats to cut down on dust. Clean wood shavings are acceptable as bedding. Shredded paper may also be used as a substitute for straw or shavings and will not generate as much dust. The horse should be housed in an area with good ventilation, and his stall should be kept clean, as ammonia will irritate his lungs.

To help cut down on stable-dust sources, spray hay with water. If hay has to be eliminated from the horse's diet, substitute wet beet pulp or wet alfalfa cubes, provided the horse's system can tolerate the calcium content. To cut down on grain dust, feed pelleted and extruded feeds.

Horses with mild to moderate COPD have a decent chance of recovery with good care and the removal of environmental triggers. Talk to your vet about the treatments available to relieve the symptoms of heaves. Corticosteroids can soothe inflammation, bronchodilators can alleviate acute bronchial spasms, and expectorants can help to keep air passages clear.

Worst-Case Scenario: Euthanasia

Due to illness or injury, there will come a time when the light in a horse's eyes has died and he has no interest in food, play, or companionship. There is no longer any hope for a decent quality of life, let alone a return to health. Though it is hard to let go, beyond a certain point an owner cannot responsibly allow a horse to suffer any more.

Witnessing the euthanasia of a beloved horse is a distressing ordeal. Horses go down hard. Because of the potential for injury, the owner will probably not be allowed to touch the horse or offer comfort, once the drugs have taken effect. Though technically brain-dead less than a minute after the vet administers an overdose of anesthetic, the horse may thrash around for a time. If an owner can't bear to be present when euthanasia is performed, it may be best if a trusted friend or relative fills in.

If the horse is to be buried on the property, hire a backhoe in advance. Check with the local health department to make sure that it is legal to bury a horse on private property.

If the horse cannot be buried on the property and no other facilities are available, a rendering company must be called so that the remains can be removed as quickly as possible by truck. Have a tarp ready to cover the remains until the truck arrives. The euthanasia must take place in an area that is accessible to the truck. Rendering companies usually charge a small fee for picking up a horse. It is less traumatic if the owner is not present when the truck comes to pick up the horse.

Hopefully, the owner has had enough time with the horse to have accumulated an album full of happy memories. There is also some comfort in preserving a lock of the mane or tail for a remembrance. But in the end, the knowledge that the owner provided the best life possible for the horse during their time together may be the greatest source of comfort.

References and Sources of Additional Information

Freeman, David W., PhD., and Carolynn MacAllister. Oklahoma Cooperative Extension, "Fact Sheet #F-3921 Understanding Colic in Horses," December 13, 2004 www.osuextra.com.

Giffen, James, MD., and Tome Gore. *Horse Owner's Veterinary Handbook,* 2nd Edition, Howell Book House, 1998.

Lavoie, Jean-Pierre. "Heaves: Equine COPD," *Horse Country Vet Rap*, www.horse-country.com/vet/heaves.html (accessed April 5, 2004).

Rains, Jerry R., and Frank Lockner. Oklahoma Cooperative Extension Service, "Fact Sheet # F-9115 Laminitis in Horses," www.osuextra.com.

Ralston, Sarah. Dept. of Animal Sciences, Rutgers Cooperative Extension. "Fact Sheet #FS715 Management of Old Horses," August 1, 1993, and "#FS073: Forage Substitutes for Horses," February 17, 2000, www.rutgers.edu (accessed February 15, 2004).

Ramey, David W. *Medications & Supplements for the Horse*, Howell Book House, 1996.

4

Disposition, Behavior, and Training

First impressions of your new horse in his new home may make you wonder what you have gotten yourself into. Ideally, a calm, well-trained horse should not forget his manners in a different environment. But the reality is that many horses do not appreciate a sudden change of address and will be somewhat excitable the first few days. After the new horse has had some time to settle down, you can make a better evaluation of his disposition and training.

Pay close attention to equine body language, especially if you are unfamiliar with the horse's past treatment. A normal horse, handled by conscientious, kindly people, will face you with his ears forward, head level, and will have a pleasant, hopeful expression on his face. After receiving his food and water, he will dig right in, and, although he may check you out occasionally, will not show much concern regarding your presence.

Evaluating a New Horse

There is no such thing as a "good horse" or a "bad horse." Horses are animals and have no concept of morals. Good horses do not attend

This friendly little horse has a definite feeling of entitlement.

church regularly, and bad horses do not mug unwary travelers for carrots on dark country roads. Horses have limited reasoning ability, and they are mentally incapable of premeditated evil. Horses do not even have a clear concept of self, let alone the ability to understand how their actions affect others. Subsequently, equine misbehavior should never be taken personally.

One example of taking equine behavior personally is the commonly held belief that some horses hate men. A horse may have negative associations with certain male characteristics, if a man has abused him in the past. This is because he has been conditioned to associate a deeper voice or assertive behavior with bad experiences. Such negative conditioning may take time to overcome. However, a skilled horse trainer can generally overcome negative conditioning and a supposed equine preference for either sex.

Hollywood's romanticized and humanized image of the horse has resulted in unrealistic expectations. Movie horse behaviors, such as counting, nodding *yes* in response to questions, and running through a hail of bullets to save his owner, do not come naturally to a horse. Movie horse tricks are the result of months, even years, of skillful, patient training.

Unrealistic expectations can lead to cruelty when humans take equine misbehavior personally and expect too much, too soon of a simple animal. For the most part, horses misbehave because they are frightened, in pain, and don't understand what human beings want from them. Instinct governs most of their actions, especially the flight instinct, which is necessary for the survival of any prey animal. Instinct tells them to run first and ask questions later.

Some horses are timid and excitable most of the time, while others are calm and collected. However, the same horse can behave like a bombproof babysitter or a cowardly claustrophobic, depending on the circumstances. Much of a horse's outward behavior is a result of training—or lack of it.

This section of the book includes procedures that you can use to evaluate a horse's previous training. Training tips and general approaches to solving behavior problems are also included, but you must recognize when a horse is too much to handle before trying any of these methods.

When a horse violently resists any effort at control and cannot be safely handled without risking injury to both animal and handler, professional help is required. Only a competent professional, with years of experience and a toolbox full of different training methods, may possess the knowledge to safely retrain a horse made dangerous by incompetent handling or outright abuse.

Horses are forgiving souls, and even severely abused horses can eventually be taught to trust human beings, but only if they are expertly and patiently handled. Be realistic concerning your own abilities. Do not let a cowboy attitude and a ten-gallon ego get you in trouble. If you feel intimidated by a horse in any given situation, get help! Your ego will heal faster than your body if a rowdy horse does a tap dance on your skull.

This section on training is meant as a road map, not a manual. Much of horse training is subjective and cannot be learned from a book. I have no way of knowing your skill level or the amount of patience you have. You have to do any training task with a horse at least five times before you can expect to make any progress at all. The amount of patience you have is probably the most important horse-training tool you possess. Novices can accomplish amazing things with horses through patience, time, and love, but knowledge from mentors is also important. The road signs provided in this book will tell you which direction to go, but how you get to your destination is entirely up to you.

Checking for Areas of Resistance

The following procedures will give you some indication of your new horse's previous training experiences. Doing your own evaluation is much safer than relying on seller information.

Pick a quiet time of day to evaluate your horse's disposition and previous handling. Things will also work out better if the horse has had some pasture time instead of being kept in a locked stall all day.

Outfit the horse with a halter and lead rope. Then methodically go over the parts of his body looking for areas where he is overly sensitive or resistant to pressure.

Vertical Flexion

Starting with the head, place your hand on the bridge of the nose and exert gentle pressure with the tips of your fingers. The horse should tip his head slightly and give to the pressure. A few sensitive horses will bend their necks and even back up in response to gentle pressure on the bridge of the nose. Finger pressure works better than using the flat of your hand. Release the pressure as soon as the horse gives.

This horse is backing up in response to gentle pressure on the bridge of the nose.

Move back behind the ears to exert gentle pressure on the top of the horse's neck. See if he will drop his head in response to downward pressure from your hand. Horses that give to pressure on the top of the neck and bridge of the nose are less likely to have problems with vertical flexion under saddle, and they are more likely to give to bit and rein pressure and stay collected.

The ideal response is calm, sensitive yielding to pressure. Many laid-back, gentle horses will not respond much at all, whereas a sensitive, excitable horse may overreact. Resistance, such as tossing the head or pushing back, does not necessarily mean that the horse is stubborn or insensitive. A horse's natural instinct is to push against pressure. Most horses have to be trained to give to pressure. This is

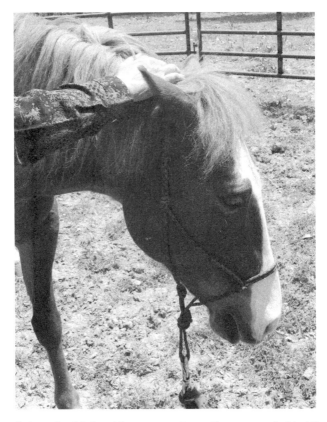

This horse is lowering his head in response to gentle pressure behind the ears.

done by exerting only as much pressure as will elicit a correct response, no matter how slight, then removing the pressure as a reward.

Lateral Flexion

See how far you can get the horse to bend his head and neck around without moving his back legs. A horse that bends his neck easily in response to lead rope pressure is more likely to have power steering once you pick up the reins.

Yielding the Forehand

If you stand to the side, and slightly in front of the horse, and gently press on the jaw and girth area, does he yield his forehand or try to keep walking forward? A horse should be trained to yield his forehand in either direction while being led, to keep him from walking on top of you. Yielding the forehand helps when operating gates and is a basic part of many dressage maneuvers.

This horse is yielding his forehand.

Yielding the Hindquarters

Lightly press your fingers into the horse's flank (see photos below) to see if he will move his hindquarters over for you. Horses that yield their hindquarters easily should be more responsive to leg cues from a rider. Horses that yield these body areas in response to pressure are safer to work around in close quarters, and they are less likely to crowd their owners.

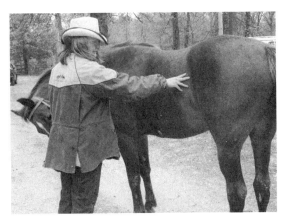

Exerting pressure on the flank area should cause a horse to yield his hindquarters.

This horse is yielding his hindquarters in response to pressure on the flank area.

Handling the Head

Handling the Ears

Stroke the horse's forehead. Move your hand back and lightly stroke over the top of the horse's ears. Extreme sensitivity around the ears may indicate chronic head shyness, lack of handling, or experience with rough bridling methods in the past.

Exercise caution when bridling a head-shy horse for the first time, especially if the horse is tied. Extremely head-shy horses can pull back hard enough to break a halter and lead rope, or even rear up and go over backwards in a claustrophobic effort to escape.

Unless the horse is extremely wild, or simply being disrespectful, you may be able to desensitize the horse to having his ears handled by gently and quickly stroking from the horse's forehead, over the tops of his ears with your hands, until he starts to relax and accept the attention. Make a point of doing this once or twice each day at feeding time, or when you are giving him a treat.

Desensitizing a horse to having his ears handled.

Extremely wild or disrespectful horses may require preliminary round-pen and other ground schooling focused on controlling their movements and teaching them to stand still, before ear desensitization can be successfully completed.

Carefully stroke the horse's lips and muzzle, inserting your thumb in the interdental gap between the incisors and molars. See if you can get him to open his mouth. Run your fingers up under his front lip and massage his gums.

A horse that shows a lot of resistance to being handled around the mouth may also have trouble accepting the bit.

If you can't bridle the horse without a fight, think twice about riding him without some additional training. Potential resistance may not be confined to bridling problems.

Handling the Body

Check for Sore Spots

Gently rub and probe along each side of the horse's spine, starting with the neck, all the way down to the tail head. Feel for lumps, bumps, and warmth. Some of the more sensitive horses will sink down in the back the first time they are subjected to this treatment, but if they show continued discomfort, a veterinary examination is in order.

Handling the Tail and Gaskin Area

Lightly brush your hand over the tail and down to the hocks. If the horse clamps his tail down, he has not been fully desensitized to having his tail handled. Be careful. The hamstring is located in the area above the hocks and below the tail head. Since the hamstring is a favorite target of predators in the wild, handling this area may inspire the kicking reflex in an excitable horse.

If the horse remains calm when you brush your hand over the tail head, see how the he reacts to having his tail handled. Stand at the horse's side, and be ready to back off if he threatens to kick. While standing near the girth area, reach over, and pull the tail around towards you. The horse should remain unconcerned.

Saddle Area Sensitivity

Using the tips of your fingers, stroke the horse's sides, starting at the girth area, back to the flanks. Excitable horses may threaten to kick if you touch the loin area. If the horse is really goosey, you may expect a negative reaction when the stirrup leathers or your legs touch those areas when you are riding him. Stroke underneath the belly and girth area. If the horse is unusually sensitive in this area, you may have problems the first time you cinch him up. He may shy away or kick at your hand.

Horses need to be desensitized to the pressure of a girth strap in preparation for saddling. If the lead rope is long enough, wrap one end around the horse's girth area and exert gentle pressure. If the horse switches his tail and becomes disturbed at gentle rope pressure, you can probably expect some problems when you cinch him up for the first time.

More Ticklish Areas

If the horse is a stallion or gelding, see if the genital area can be handled, which will be important in maintaining health and hygiene. If the animal is a mare, see if the udder can be handled safely. Be careful, as horses not previously handled in these areas may shy away or try to kick.

Handling the Legs and Feet

A horse that switches his tail rapidly and stamps his back feet may be preparing to kick. Work near his shoulder area, and keep out of striking range. You can safely test for kicking behavior by using the soft end of a lunge whip to gently stroke his legs and stomach. If he kicks at the whip, there's a good chance he might kick you. You can also test kicking tendencies by gently swinging a soft rope against his hind legs. Be sure to desensitize the horse to the presence of ropes or whips in his general vicinity before attempting to touch him with these objects, or you may get a violent reaction.

If the horse has remained calm up to this point, use your hands to rub and stroke each one of the legs, slowly working your way down. Lightly pinch the tendon running along the back of the legs to pick up each one of the feet. You should be able to pick up and hold each foot for several seconds without the horse trying to pull away. Pat the bottoms of the horse's feet with the bottoms of your hands, or gently tap the soles of the feet with a hammer. The horse should remain calm. Gently lower each hoof to the ground when you are done. How the horse reacts to having his legs and feet handled is important, as he will need to stand quietly for regular foot care by you as well as the farrier.

How to handle a horse that shies away or threatens to kick when you try to handle his legs depends on whether the problem is fear-based or stems from lack of respect. Fear-based resistance generally is improved by an advance-and-retreat approach.

If the horse shies away from having his legs handled out of fear, and even threatens to kick, stay out of reach by gently rubbing the horse's legs with the end of a lunge whip for starters. Then slowly work your way down the leg, rewarding the horse each time he accepts your actions calmly by stepping back and removing the pressure, then petting and praising him. Finally, you would pick the horse's feet up for brief periods of time, and setting them back down gently, until the horse learns to accept having his feet handled.

A horse with respect issues needs training methods focused on teaching him that it is pleasant to stand still and a lot more work to misbehave. Groundwork maneuvers that help foster respect, such as motivating the horse to yield his hindquarters and back up, can help. Round-pen work is another way to control a horse's movements. If done correctly, round-pen work will teach a horse to stand quietly and pay attention to his handler.

Changing Eyes

Holding the lead rope in one hand, move the horse's head left or right with the other, until you are standing on the opposite side of his head. Or, leaving your hand on his nose, physically walk from one side of his body to the other. Be careful doing this, as you are moving in and out of the blind spot directly in front of the horse's nose. Some horses will become so disturbed by this maneuver that they will try to run over you.

What you are checking for is a horse's ability to "switch eyes" or "change eyes." Horses have both monocular vision and binocular vision. Horses have to switch from monocular vision (focusing with one eye) to binocular (focusing with two eyes) in order to see objects more clearly. They also have blind spots directly in front of the nose and behind their tails.

To make things even more interesting, what a horse sees with his right eye may not automatically be recognized by the left, which is why trainers desensitize both sides of a horse and spend so much time sacking a colt out during training. The part of a horse's brain that transfers information from one side to the other is poorly developed. The horse needs to be properly conditioned to be able to switch information from the right eye to the left eye without panicking.

A horse that becomes extremely defensive on one side of his body has not had sufficient desensitization training. A horse like this is not safe to ride, unless you always sit straight as a poker, never wave at your friends, and never try to get on or off your horse. This last part is especially important, because a horse who can't "switch eyes" can get upset when someone throws a leg across his back.

Sacking Out

Sacking out is the process of desensitizing a horse to having a saddle blanket, paper bag, or some other object rubbed all over his body and waved around in and out of blind spots until he accepts its pressure calmly. Every horse should have been thoroughly sacked out as a part of basic training. A horse that has not been sacked out can be dangerous to ride. To check if the horse has been adequately desensitized, stand at the horse's shoulder, take a saddle pad and gently rub it over the horse's back, withers, rump, and both of his sides. Start slowly, allowing the horse time to sniff and examine the saddle pad before laying it across his back. Continue on down to his legs. Be careful to keep your head out of kicking range while doing the back legs. If you encounter a lot of resistance at any point in the process, the horse has some significant gaps in his training.

Horses can be sacked out with all kinds of objects. Note the extremely alert posture of the horse in the first picture below. His head is elevated and the neck muscles are tense, ears are pointed far forward, nostrils are flared, and tail is clamped tightly to his rump. He is preparing to run. Using an advance-and-retreat approach, the handler eventually desensitizes the horse to having the umbrella in his vicinity, then rubbed all over his body, until he is unconcerned by its presence.

Horses can be sacked out using all kinds of objects, including umbrellas.

Saddling Up

The horse should accept bridling and saddling calmly. It is not advisable to step up on a horse that is switching his tail and attempting to bite before you even put a foot in the stirrup. He should also remain quiet and unconcerned while you are mounting. Behave as though you were mounting a green-broke horse. Bounce up and down on the stirrup a few times, and lean over the saddle, before actually committing yourself to mounting.

The horse should stand quietly, on a loose rein, until you actually tell him to go somewhere. He should walk, trot, and canter when asked. He should also stop, turn right and left, and back up when asked. He should do all this calmly, in and out of the arena.

Extreme fear or extreme aggression during handling with blankets, pads, or ropes, may be a sign of previous abuse. Animal abusers, masquerading as horse trainers, will hog-tie a colt and beat him into a stupor with tarps, ropes, or whips. The object is to break the animal's spirit. This kind of treatment often results in a severely traumatized horse. Horses subjected to such extreme training methods can become violent if a human attempts to touch their bodies with any object, especially behind the withers. Horses displaying extremely fearful or aggressive behavior should be handled by professional trainers or highly experienced owners—not beginners.

Abusive training will occasionally "succeed" in producing a horse that is well-behaved and buttoned-down, even robotic. But such a horse may lapse into an unresponsive, hypnotic stupor when under stress. His entire body may go completely tense and rigid, every muscle hard as a rock. The horse is not just balking, though the body stance is similar. The horse is in a state of shock, akin to the condition of an animal in a predator's jaws that has given up all hope of escape. The horse must be allowed to recover in peace and quiet, in a safe area. Otherwise, a massive surge of adrenaline may immediately follow the stupor, and send him crashing through the nearest fence.

Abusive methods of horse training often result from ignorance, and pressure from owners to get training results in a very short time.

Competent trainers can spend years to trying to undo the damage an incompetent trainer can do in just thirty days. Steer clear of bargain-basement horse trainers, especially the ones that don't want you around while your horse is being worked.

Warning Signs: Equine Body Language

The following equine body language indicates excitement or displeasure with being handled.

Fear: Body trembling; ears held in an extremely tense, forward position, or pinned tightly to the head; bulging, white-rimmed eyes; high head; tensely muscled neck; extremely high tail carriage or tail clamped to rump; flared nostrils; shying away from contact.

Anger: Pinned ears; stony eye; bared teeth; tensely arched neck; flared nostrils; snorting, grunting, and growling noises; squealing; rapidly switching tail; pawing; and stomping the front and back feet.

Animals with a history of abuse are quite capable of rearing, kicking, biting, or striking out of fear. A professional trainer, not a beginner, should deal with extremely aggressive or extremely wild behavior.

Handling Problem Horses

Leading

When you lead the horse, does he forge ahead, pulling you along behind? Or do you have to drag him along behind like a giant pull-toy? Either way, the horse has not been taught to give to pressure, so he probably will not be very responsive to cues from the saddle if or when you decide to ride him.

A rope halter may help (see photo below). Rope halters exert more pressure on a smaller area, and they also have artfully placed knots at sensitive areas on the bridge of a horse's nose. Bitless side-pulls (see photo) are another option and also provide increased pressure on the bridge of the nose. Chains across the nose are not the best solution. If the horse breaks away from the handler and steps on the lead rope, the chain will cut the horse's nose.

Rope halter   Bitless side-pull

Head shyness, resistance to haltering, and pulling against the lead rope, are signs of a substandard training history. Be cautious about leaving such a horse tied and unsupervised. A horse that has not been taught to give to pressure from a lead rope may resort to extreme behaviors such as rearing, falling over backwards, or pulling back and breaking the halter or lead rope when left tied for any length of time.

Note: To correct leading problems such as forging ahead of the handler or pulling on the handler, the handler will have to teach the horse to respond to pressure from the lead rope. Horses need to learn that if they respond to gentle pressure on a lead rope, they are rewarded by release from that pressure.

Strategies that may also help with leading problems include teaching a horse to yield his hindquarters, turn on the forehand, and back up. Teaching a horse to tip his head towards you and yield his hindquarters helps to slow him down in the case of a horse that forges ahead. Backing a horse up after asking him to yield his hindquarters also helps the horse that forges ahead of you to think about stopping.

In the case of a horse that balks, yielding the hindquarters gets his feet moving. It is also more effective to drive a balking horse from the rear than to engage in a tug-of-war.

When trying to work with a horse who has not been taught to lead, it may be more effective to use a longer lead rope. Work opposite the horse's shoulder, where you can exert more leverage, step to one side, and pull. When the horse responds, give him some slack. The horse may end up circling around you quite a bit before he finally learns to lead. Horses who have not been taught to lead should be worked in a corral or other confined space.

Shyness

A horse that hasn't been handled much, or has been abused, will move to the back of the stall when you approach. He may even tremble noticeably if you stare directly at him for any length of time. Such horses have not been taught to relax around humans. It will take some time to acclimate him to your presence. Go get a good book and a bucket to sit on, and hang out by the stall door for a while.

Don't face the horse directly. Don't stare at him like he is something good to eat. Remember that horses are prey animals and that kind of behavior coming from any predator, including humans, tends to make them uncomfortable. Sit or stand with your shoulder towards him. Give the horse time to come up and investigate you on his own. If he does come over to you, invite him to smell the back of your hand as a way of introduction. Bribery may also help. If you don't like to hand-feed a horse, offer him some treats out of a bucket, or walk in and out of his area periodically to toss a goody in the feed box.

Always approach a nervous horse, or any strange horse, from the side, and stand shoulder to shoulder. Many horses don't like to be approached directly from the front. Horses generally approach one another from the side, and you don't want to appear confrontational. Also, they simply can't see you all that clearly when you approach directly from the front, because their eyes are set on the sides, and they have a blind spot in front of their faces. Ditto for approaching a nervous horse from the rear; they can't see you very well back there, and they may decide to kick first and ask questions later.

It also helps to spend time just walking along beside a nervous horse while he is grazing in the pasture. Don't stare at him. Walk slowly, with your head down, and your shoulder towards him, on a parallel course with his movements. When he accepts your presence and drops his head to graze, just stand there for a while and let him relax before trying to move in closer.

Don't try to catch the horse. Just spend some time hanging out, standing quietly while he grazes, and slowly decrease the distance you are standing from him, walking at his shoulder. When he finally becomes comfortable with your presence, reach out and rub him in back of the withers.

The Hard-to-catch Horse:

If the only time you catch your horse is when you want to work him, he will be that much harder to catch the next time. Make a point of going out there just to visit, offer bribes or a nice shoulder rub, and just leave. Walk in and out of the pasture several times a day, and just don't do anything. Don't even look at him. Habituate him to your presence.

Play with one of the other horses and ignore him entirely. If the other horses accept your presence, he may soon become curious about you and come up to investigate. Remember that he is a prey animal. Try not to give him the idea that you are always out to get him. When you do catch him, let him graze on the tender grass in your yard while you brush him, so that he associates pleasant activities with being caught.

Use other horses to catch the shy one. If you are trying to catch a horse in a large pasture with other horses, you can catch the dominant horse of the herd first, and lead him into a smaller enclosure. Hopefully, the other horses in the herd will follow you.

Unfortunately, one of the reasons a horse is hard to catch may be the presence of a more dominant horse in the herd. The dominant horse may drive the more passive animal off in an attempt to get all the treats and attention. Bringing a bucket of grain into a herd of horses can be dangerous, as you can end up in the middle of an equine food fight.

Though you can't change the pecking order, you can discourage more-dominant horses from interfering when you are trying to work with a less-dominant horse. It is very important that you teach each horse in the herd to respect your space individually before attempting to work with horses in a group.

Use caution when working with horses in a group. Learn to control them individually first.

Round-pen work and other groundwork methods will help. Do not allow dominant horses to crowd you. Establish the meaning of a voice command such as "Back off!" and head toward the horse's chest with determined body language and a twirling lead rope until he does back off. Take a lead rope into the pasture and herd the dominant horse by putting pressure on the flank area with a spinning lead rope and driving from the rear, being careful to stay out of kicking range.

It is very important that you establish yourself as the "boss horse" in a herd situation. We all want to be kind to our animals and want our horses to like us, but horses actually think more of handlers that have the ability to establish authority without causing pain. Horses look to the boss member of the herd for survival, and they will actually be happier and less fearful in your company if you take the dominant position and establish some ground rules for behavior.

The boss or alpha member of the herd makes the other horses feel safe and secure. Security is very important to horses. Less-dominant horses willingly submit to aggressive herding behavior from the alpha horse. They have entrusted their survival to his leadership and will follow him anywhere.

In a human/horse herd, the human needs to take the place of the alpha horse. Round-pen training can help make this possible. If round-pen training is done correctly, the horse accepts human leadership, and he comes to believe that the best and safest place to be is right beside his trainer.

Barn-Sour Behavior

A new horse may associate the barn and other horses with security. Unfortunately, this need for security can cause problems. A timid, fearful horse may not want to leave the company of other horses until he trusts and respects the leadership of his owner.

Strategies that convince the horse that there are advantages to having his owner all to himself may help. Ride the horse over to a friendly neighbor's house and allow him to graze when you get there. Or just take the horse for a walk at the end of a lead rope, and let him stop to graze on the tender grass in your yard. Find ways to reward him for good behavior while you increase the distance from his security zone.

When riding a barn-sour horse, if you can't get the horse's feet to move in the direction you want, just get his feet to move. Tip his head toward one side, get his feet to move in a circle, and swing back around in the direction you want to go. Find something for him to do, such as serpentines around obstacles. Occupy his mind with something else besides resistance. Work him on the way home. Convince him that it is much easier just to head in the direction you want to go. Remember that one of the most important principles of horse training is to make the right thing easy and the wrong thing difficult.

When you get home, don't immediately put him back in the stall or pasture with his buddies. Put him to work right next to the barn.

If the horse wants to bolt, pull his head around in the opposite direction, and ask the horse to yield his hindquarters. Learn to execute a one-rein stop in a safe, confined area before hitting the trails on a horse with a tendency to bolt. Make sure you get his attention on the ground as well, by teaching him to yield his hindquarters and give you his attention at the end of a lead rope with more groundwork, with emphasis on teaching him to yield to pressure.

With time and patience, most barn-sour behavior can be overcome. Though some overly timid horses never really relax outside their own home turf, they can be trained to trust their rider and become obedient under tense circumstances. Barn-sour horses do have one big advantage for backcountry trail riders. It is harder to get lost on a barn-sour horse, because they have an excellent sense of direction and always seem to know the way home.

Aggression

Biting

Biting is a common form of aggression that can vary in seriousness from gently mouthing an owner's shirt, to a horse that pins his ears and lunges at every visitor, mouth wide open, with the obvious intention of severing an appendage. The latter case should only be dealt with by professionals or highly experienced owners. Be sure to put up a stall guard and warn potential visitors off! Dangerously aggressive horses should never be housed in high-traffic areas.

Reasons for biting vary. Young horses often nip because they are teething, much the same way a teething human child will gnaw on things because it feels better. Once they reach the age of two, many young horses simply outgrow the need to nibble on their owners. However, biting is a training issue that needs to be addressed. Even if your big baby doesn't mean it personally, he should not be allowed to mistake his owner for a chew toy.

Other horses make the mistake of thinking that human beings actually enjoy mutual grooming sessions with those big piano key–size teeth, just like their horse buddies. Or they think their owner wants to play. Of course most horses have no idea how thin-skinned human beings really are. That is why your horse has the nerve to look surprised and offended when a desperate little human fist lands on his muzzle.

Some horses have territorial issues regarding their stalls. New horses, stressed out by the presence of unfamiliar horses and people, sometimes react this way. Such horses can get especially aggressive at feeding time. The new horse behaves as though the very same human providing him with breakfast in bed intends to drive him off and steal his grain. Anyone approaching the stall door will be met with pinned ears and bite threats. Curing the problem is difficult and will take some time and effort.

Threatening the horse with a shovel may only teach him to wait until your back is turned before going after you. Besides, resorting to violence will only reinforce the horse's paranoid belief that you are trying to drive him away.

A safer and more humane method to discourage such behavior is to take the butt of a lunge whip and exert gentle, steady pressure against the base of his neck or chest until he backs off. If the horse is extremely aggressive, do this with a closed stall door, gate, or fence as an obstacle between you.

The best time to start training is when the feed box is empty. As soon as he backs up to a safe distance, throw some sort of small treat, such as a piece of carrot, in his feed box. Then step back and allow the horse to approach the feed box. As soon as the horse sticks his nose in the box to eat the goody (as opposed to trying to eat you), say "good boy" and voice your approval. When he is done with the treat, repeat the whole process until the horse starts to understand that respectful behavior is rewarded. You are accomplishing several things by using this method of positive reinforcement.

You are keeping yourself safe, because this method can be employed from a safe distance, with a stall door between you and the horse. You are reassuring the horse that you are not there to drive him out of his stall or away from his food and that your visits have pleasant results, as long as he respects your space. You are also directing the horse's attention toward the feed box and away from the front of his stall. By praising the horse for doing something he likes to do anyway—consuming treats—you are teaching him that the phrase "good boy" is an indication that he has done the right thing, thereby opening a line of communication.

Putting grain in the horse's feed box before you bring him in out of the pasture will also help to reduce tension. If you have really good-quality hay and pasture, you might talk to your vet about cutting out grain altogether and feeding more hay. This may be an extreme measure, but if the horse is really dangerous over this issue, you might want to consider this option. Horses are not inclined to be as protective over hay. Grain is more of a treat.

Another way to discourage biting is to hide a small squirt bottle of water or lemon juice in your hand. The bottle should be small enough that he doesn't see it, because you don't want him to know where the spray is coming from. When the horse tries to bite, squirt him in the nose.

If the horse is not too aggressive about biting, you can use the situation to your advantage. Since he is determined to shove his big nose in your face anyway, take the side of the halter firmly in your hand and carefully proceed with desensitization training of his mouth and muzzle. Use your hand to stroke down each side of his muzzle, stick your fingers in the interdental gap and inspect his teeth, clean his nose, or whatever else you can think of.

To treat or not to treat? A horse can get aggressive and pushy over treats. The obvious answer is not to give him any.

The paint pickpocket on the handler's right eventually turned to a life of crime to support his carrot habit.

The alternative is to provide treats from a bucket or toss them in his feed box, although you can teach a horse to be polite about treats. Every time you offer the horse a treat, exert gentle pressure on his neck, right behind the ears, and hold the treat down so that he has to drop his head down low to get it. That way, you are rewarding submissive behavior, not pushy behavior. You can also exert pressure on the bridge of his nose, and get him to back up first, before offering a treat. Keep repeating the action until the horse associates submissive behavior with getting a treat.

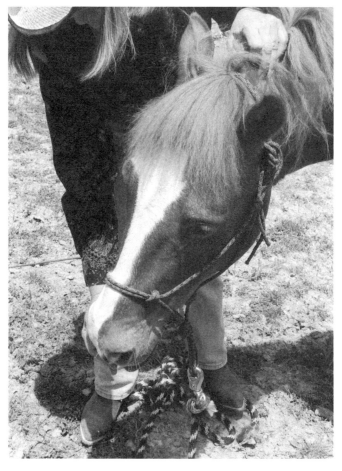

Ask a horse to lower his head by exerting gentle pressure behind the ears while offering a treat in order to encourage respect.

Territorial Kicking

A horse that greets you rump first when you come in the stall may be ready for a fight. A horse who pins his ears back, switches his tail irritably, and cocks a back foot is definitely telling you to talk to the hoof. You are in imminent danger of being kicked. Swing a lead rope at his hindquarters or tap him on the side of the hip with a lunge whip until he turns to face you, and stay out of reach. Reward and praise him when he turns to face you.

Teaching him to yield his hindquarters and face you may help. Put a halter and a long lead rope (at least 12 feet) on the horse. Stand opposite the horse's shoulder, but not too close. Stay out of kicking

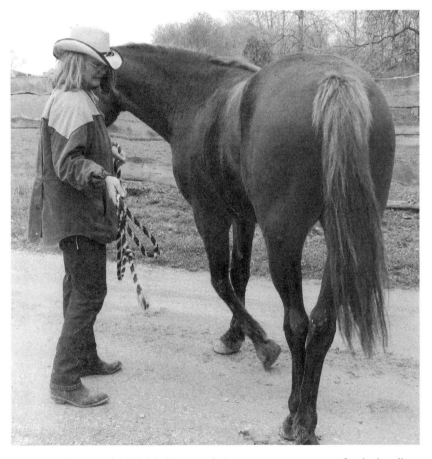

Teaching a horse to yield his hindquarters helps to encourage respect for the handler.

range. With your left hand grasping the lead rope, tip the horse's nose in your direction. Now take the remainder of the lead rope in your right hand and swing it at the horse's hip. He should step over and yield his hindquarters away from you. Since dominant horses in a herd will drive another horse from the rear, he will recognize the body language. Head toward his flank like you mean business. Round-pen techniques are also useful in teaching respect at a safe distance. Kicking is a dangerous vice, and an owner should not hesitate to seek expert help when needed.

Disrespecting Your Space

A horse that shoves you aside with his shoulder or steps on your feet while you are leading him may not be overly aggressive by nature, just a product of poor training. He has never been taught to respect a human's space. You can keep him physically off of you by shoving your elbow, the

Tap a horse lightly on the neck with a whip to get him to move over and respect your space.

heel of your hand, or the butt of a whip against his neck. As you lead him along, keep your right hand up to block his movements. You can also step back away from him, and then swing the end of a long, twelve-foot lead rope at his shoulder and hip like a propeller until he steps away from you. It is better to let a horse run into some obstacle, like the butt of a whip or a twirling lead rope, than to hit him with anything.

Another way to get a horse to move over is to lift your right hand up high and make a motion at the side of the horse's face, as though you were going to push his left eye over, until he yields his forehand. Lead with your shoulder opposite the horse's throatlatch so you can reach the horse's head and neck area. Even though you don't want to hit or hurt the horse, you may have to tap him on the side of the neck with a whip if he is really determined to run you over.

Factors Affecting Equine Disposition and Behavior

Sometimes a horse's true disposition is hard to determine. Abusive training methods can make a gentle horse appear uncontrollable, whereas expert handling can make an excitable horse appear gentle. Either way, basic disposition remains the same. Outward appearances can be deceptive. The horse of your dreams may be hiding behind a grubby, terrified exterior, and your worst nightmare may be waiting, shaved and blanketed, in a stall decorated with wrought iron. Before you decide whether you can get along with a particular horse, it helps to understand some of the reasons for his behavior.

Herd Behavior

Horses are social animals and require the presence of other horses for a feeling of security. This is one of the reasons that horses are trainable. They are genetically programmed to live in a cooperative social situation and operate within a defined pecking order.

Herd dynamics influence disposition. Dominant mares raise dominant foals. A young foal learns his place in the herd hierarchy from his mother. If his mother is a calm, confident, individual, her colt will probably grow up to be that way. If she is afraid of her own shadow, the baby may also learn to be fearful. If she is a strict disciplinarian, he will grow up to be respectful. If she lets him get away with murder, he will grow up to have trouble with any authority figure, including human beings.

Horses learn to be cooperative by living in a herd. Older members of the herd soon put a young, arrogant horse in his place. Horses need the company of other horses, and human beings are a poor substitute. Keeping horses in isolation can lead to bizarre behavior due to the stress of living alone.

Isolation contributes to neurotic behaviors such as stall-weaving. Isolation can also cause a horse to become overly fearful or overly excited when finally allowed to see other horses. When horses are confined to a stall or kept alone in a paddock, they should at least have visual contact with other horses.

Synchronicity

Horses tend to adopt the attitudes of the creatures around them. Observe the behavior of horses in a herd situation when a kid on a bicycle rides by. The younger horses in the herd may become startled, especially if the cyclist is wearing one of those neon space-alien getups with matching helmet. However, if the alpha, or leader horse of the herd, accepts the appearance of this noisy apparition, the younger members will soon settle down.

When you are riding your horse, you take the place of the herd leader, and your attitude has a great deal of influence on his attitude. If you are a confident and relaxed rider, your horse will be calmer. If you start breathing faster and stiffen up in the saddle in stressful situations, your horse will pick up on your nervousness and lose confidence.

Genetics

Disposition is partially determined by characteristics horse breeders value the most. Racehorse breeders prize a competitive disposition, so they select for bloodlines with running ability. Unfortunately, breeding for speed can also result in horses with excitable temperaments. A certain percentage of racehorses are born with a permanent case of road rage, although a competitive disposition is not confined to thoroughbreds. A high degree of athleticism is often accompanied by a high-strung disposition.

On the other hand, some other breeds of horses have been specifically bred as pleasure-riding horses. Rocky Mountain horse breeders prize the qualities that make for a relaxing trail ride and have selected for smooth gaits and gentle dispositions. A relatively high percentage of Rocky Mountain horses make good babysitters.

Therefore, you probably have a better chance of finding a gentle Rocky Mountain horse for your kids—although they might find the idea of owning a racehorse much more entertaining and would probably enjoy rocketing down narrow trails at forty miles per hour.

> **Note:** Just for the record, much of racehorse behavior is determined by the fact that these horses are fed the equine equivalent of rocket fuel. Racehorse training emphasizes speed over control, but thoroughbreds are sensitive, intelligent animals, and most can be successfully retrained for other activities.
>
>

Age

Young horses can be just plain goofy at times. They haven't seen a whole lot of the world, so they are more likely to spook at unfamiliar objects than older, experienced horses. Young horses have shorter attention spans, and they may resist control out of pure playfulness. Young horses require steady, experienced handling.

Most people, especially beginners, are better off owning an older, well-trained horse. Older horses are more likely to be patient and forgiving of mistakes, and they are less likely to regard their owners as entertaining chew toys.

Sex

Hormones influence a mare's disposition. Mares come into heat monthly and are ready to breed, unless they are already pregnant. Some mares develop a severe case of equine attention deficit disorder for about seven days out of every month. Other mares show little, if any change in behavior.

Hormones also affect the disposition of stallions. Stallions are always ready to breed, and they may start acting up at the sight of a passing mare. There are exceptions, but most tend to be somewhat aggressive. They are programmed by nature to be territorial and may attack other male horses. Stallions will also try to dominate their owners and should not be handled by beginners.

Geldings tend to be more even-tempered than either stallions or mares, being rendered surgically incapable of having much interest in the opposite sex.

Vision

Horses see things differently than humans. They have a wide field of vision, but they can't see details like we do. At distances more than 100 feet away, they can't really tell if that brown lump in the grass is a bale of hay or a mountain lion getting ready to pounce. Equine depth perception is also poor, which is one reason they are so hesitant about crossing ditches and streams.

Horses can focus both eyes on an object, but their field of binocular (two-eyed) vision is roughly half of ours. In most situations, horses have to turn their heads to get a good look at something with both eyes. Equines have an extremely wide field of monocular vision (focusing one eye at a time on an object). However, monocular vision is more useful for detecting movement than recognizing details.

Monocular vision may be great for spotting sudden movements, but it can complicate horse training. Visual information from the right side of a horse's brain doesn't necessarily transfer to the left. The part of a horse's brain that transfers visual information is poorly developed.

For instance, if you pass a "horse-eating" trash can and manage to convince your horse that it is harmless, he may still shy on the way back when he views it out of the opposite eye. This is why you need to do desensitization procedures, such as sacking out a horse, on both sides of the horse's body.

Because their eyes are set on the sides of their heads, horses have blind spots located directly in front of their noses, below their heads, and directly behind their tails. Therefore, horses need the freedom to be able to lower or turn their heads to negotiate obstacles safely. For this reason, it is a good idea to allow your horse the chance to lower his head and investigate a stream before crossing, or before entering a strange trailer ramp. Your horse is not being stubborn. It's just that he needs to lower his head to see past that big old moose nose.

If a normally bombproof horse suddenly becomes paranoid and clumsy, it may be worthwhile to have his vision checked. According to some experts, at least one third of all horses may have substandard vision.

Diet and Exercise

A stir-crazy horse, confined in a stall most of the time and fed a high-carbohydrate, high-protein grain diet, can become a time bomb waiting to go off as soon as anyone opens the stall door. A horse that gets too little exercise and too much sweet feed can develop some dangerous behavior problems, such as shying at previously familiar objects. Increased jumpiness in regard to sounds and touch may also be noted.

You wouldn't put rocket fuel in a golf cart, and a lightly used pleasure horse doesn't require feed containing more than 12 percent protein. More roughage and less sweet feed are healthier for a horse's system. Feeding more hay can also help to prevent behavioral problems such as cribbing and wood chewing by keeping the horse occupied.

If weight gain is a concern, fat, such as corn oil or commercial supplements, can be added to the diet to put on weight without creating a carb monster. Increased turnout time, and other forms of exercise, will also help settle a horse back down.

Vitamin deficiencies have also been known to cause spooky behavior. Adding B_1 (thiamine), B_6 (pyridoxine), and magnesium to a horse's diet may help calm him down. During times when a horse has to be confined to a stall due to injury, supplements such as tryptophan and taurine, added to the horse's feed, may be helpful also. Tryptophan and taurine are amino acids. Trytophan is the stuff in turkey that makes you feel sleepy after a big Thanksgiving dinner.

How Pain Influences Behavior

Pain from health problems can result in bad behavior. Dental problems can be the root cause of resistance to bridling. Erupting canine teeth, or canine teeth that fail to erupt, resulting in a cyst, will also cause bit pain. Wolf teeth also cause problems and may have to be removed. A horse suffering from dental pain will show considerable discomfort with the bit in his mouth, chew and mouth the bit constantly, toss his head, and lean on the bit instead of giving to pressure.

Dental problems can lead to bitting problems. Having the teeth floated or changing bits may help. Loosening the cheekpieces and allowing the horse to carry the bit in his mouth may also help make the horse more comfortable. It is not absolutely necessary to tighten the bit until you see wrinkles in the corner of a horse's mouth. On the other hand, you don't want the bit loosely clanking against his teeth.

Sinus pain and pressure can cause a horse to toss his head. Problems can result from an infection in the root of one of the cheek teeth or when a virus penetrates the mucous membranes of the sinus. Persistent discharge from only one nostril is a tell-tale sign of sinus problems in a horse.

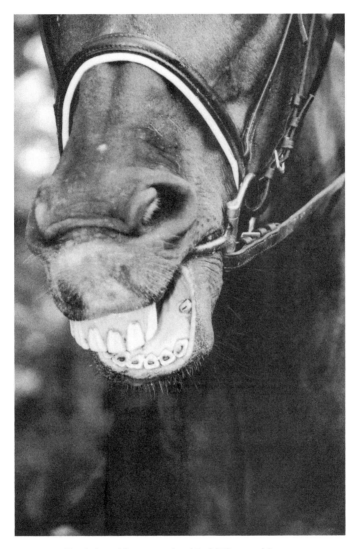

Dental problems can lead to bitting problems.

Pain from back problems, as well as soreness in any of the joints, tendons, and ligaments of the legs or feet, can cause a horse to balk, buck, or rear. When an older horse suddenly starts behaving badly, especially when he had been cooperative in the past, pain from arthritis and other health problems should be eliminated as possible causes of undesirable behavior.

Back pain from an ill-fitting saddle will cause a horse to resist going downhill. His gaits may become short and choppy because the saddle is pinching his shoulders. He will also have problems when you ask him to change gaits or change leads. The horse may even buck, rear, or bolt in an attempt to escape the pain. Saddles that are too wide in the gullet, or that are too narrow, can cause problems.

To perform a saddle-fitting check, place the saddle slightly forward of its normal position and slide it back. After finding the "sweet spot" on your horse's back, your saddle should sit level. The girth should fall a few inches behind the horse's elbow, and the saddle should settle far enough behind the horse's withers not to interfere with shoulder movement. A saddle that is placed too far forward will put pressure on the shoulders and withers.

After tightening the girth, hold the horse's head down and out of the way. Look down the gullet of the saddle. The gullet is the gap under the middle of the saddle horn or pommel, in the raised area. You should be able to see daylight at the opposite end. If you can't see all the way through, the gullet may be putting pressure on the horse's spine. There should be 2 or 3 inches of clearance between the top of the gullet and the horse's withers

Be careful of using a long-skirted Western saddle on a short-backed horse. Your saddle should only cover the ribcage, and there should be at least 4 inches between the back of the saddle and the point of the hip.

Pain from the cinch or girth can cause your horse to resist saddling. Try tightening the cinch just enough to hold the saddle on, and let him wear it a moment, walk him around a bit, then tighten it the rest of the way. Tighten the cinch slowly, by increments. Pull the cinch strap out before you pull it up. That way, the cinch ring stays away from the horse's body, and it won't wrinkle and pinch his skin.

Does your horse move away when you try to mount him? Pay attention to the way you get on your horse. Are you poking him in the ribs with those sharp-toed cowboy boots? Are you throwing so much weight against the saddle horn that you're pulling him off balance? If so, change your mounting technique. Grip the mane and back of the saddle when you mount, or turn the stirrup and swing up from the front of the saddle. If, for some physical reason, you are unable to ease yourself lightly and gently into the saddle, you might also try using a mounting block.

It only takes one rough bridling session to make a hard-to-bridle horse. Loosen the bridle before you put it on so that you do not scrunch the horse's ears down. Pull the bit up into the horse's mouth, don't just jam it in there and bump his teeth.

Take time to teach your horse to open his mouth for the bit. That way you will not clank it against his teeth when you are taking the bridle on and off. Do this by inserting a finger in the interdental gap and teaching a voice command, such as "open," to cue the horse to open his mouth.

A temporary solution for a hard-to-bridle horse is to use a halter bridle, so that the horse does not necessarily associate the bit with the bridle. That way, you can desensitize the horse to bit and bridle separately. You might also put a few drops of sweet syrup on the bit the first time you bridle the horse.

If you use a curb strap, make sure the curb strap is adjusted correctly. If you stand beside your horse and pull on the reins, you may observe the strap catching him under the chin and forcing his head up. A curb strap will make a horse throw his head up if it is not used correctly, and so will rough hands on the reins.

You should be able to insert two fingers between the horse's chin and the curb strap. That way there is more of a delay between the time that rein pressure activates the bit and the curb strap engages. Replacing a chain curb with leather can make your horse more comfortable, as will using a wider leather strap as opposed to a narrow one.

Try changing bits, especially if your horse is constantly chewing and mouthing the bit and showing other signs of discomfort. If you are riding with a broken bit, try one with a limited-travel mouthpiece or a solid mouthpiece. If you're riding with long shanks, try shorter shanks. If you are using a snaffle bit, you might want to try one with a dog bone in the middle. Dog bone bits won't poke a shallow-mouthed horse in the roof of the mouth as much as a regular snaffle.

A snaffle bit with a "dog bone" metal piece in the middle is easier on a horse's mouth.

You can also readjust the bit. Though manuals often advise tightening the bridle until the bit makes a wrinkle in the corner of the horse's mouth, many horses do better when the bit is adjusted so that there is no tension at all on the corners of the mouth. Of course, the rider must know how to use his hands once the horse has been properly bitted. And the horse must be properly trained in order to get the correct response.

How Training Influences Behavior

People often think how nice it would be to have a cute little colt around the place. But many of them don't think to start lead-breaking the baby when he weighs ninety pounds. Two years later, they wind up with a full-grown stallion bouncing around at the end of a lead rope like a 1,200-pound marlin.

A young horse needs to learn early on that a human being can control his movements. This conditioning must be accomplished with firmness, but without causing pain. Pain has a negative influence on behavior and learning. Horses do not learn well when they are in pain.

For a horse to behave correctly, he must be taught to trust human beings, as well as respect them. A horse that hasn't been conditioned to trust human leadership will trust his survival instincts instead and bolt at the first sign of danger. A horse that has not been taught to respect human beings will not give you his full attention or respect your space. Horses need to be trained mentally, physically, and emotionally in order to maintain successful partnerships with their human riders.

That's what professional horse trainers are paid to do, and professional training certainly influences a horse's behavior. But thirty days with any trainer is only the beginning of a horse's education, and it is the equine equivalent of kindergarten. Furthermore, if a horse owner spends money to hire a trainer for thirty days, then turns the colt out to pasture and forgets about him for the next six months, the money is wasted. Most young horses will eventually revert to a virtually untrained condition if not worked on a regular schedule.

Unless the horse owner has some training expertise, the horse will probably need to go back to the trainer for the occasional tune-up. Every horse owner needs to know something about training, but finding the right mentor can be a problem. Many horse trainers just don't want to deal with owners.

Trainers who advocate natural horsemanship or resistance-free training techniques will often work with both horse and rider. Resistance-free training methods have become more popular in the last few years, and they are based on relating to horses as they relate to one another in a herd situation. Resistance-free training methods use horse psychology to train horses, as opposed to more forceful training methods. According to Dan Bowman, natural horsemanship clinician, "The definition of natural horsemanship is learning to think like a horse. Resistance-free training methods focus on training the horse physically, mentally, and emotionally." Additional information on natural horsemanship techniques and Dan Bowman's methods is included in Appendix I at the back of this book.

5

Saying Good-bye: Finding a New Home for Your Horse

Horse people spend a great deal of time just taking care of their animals. Many full days are spent at the barn doing horsekeeping chores, along with riding and training. A great deal of quality time is spent just bonding with the animal. Owning a horse is a big responsibility, and horses live for a very long time. Deep emotional bonds develop between horse and owner, and separation can be traumatic. Saying good-bye to the horse that grew up with you, or who got old with you, can break your heart.

Though the owner might want to keep a horse until the animal dies of old age, this is not always possible. A lost job, failed marriage, or bad health may force the sale of a beloved companion. If the horse is well trained, young, and in good health, it is not so difficult to find a home. But what if the horse is elderly and has health issues a new owner wouldn't want to deal with? What if the horse has behavioral problems that require expert handling?

The following will offer possible solutions to the problem of finding a good home for horses with health and safety issues. Options such as leasing and donating horses to rescue organizations will be explored. A list of horse rescue facilities and adoption programs are included in Appendix II.

Horse sellers should be aware of the fact that horse buyers often become somewhat delusional where their horsemanship abilities are concerned. Some of these people honestly believe they can handle a wild mustang just because they didn't fall off an old equine pensioner twenty years ago at riding camp.

Buyers may fall in love with a horse's good looks, and they don't want to hear any warnings about training issues. Rank amateurs end up with young, excitable horses that they are unable to handle. If an amateur gets hurt, he is unlikely to place blame on his own lack of experience. The "bad horse" is soon sold at the nearest livestock sale.

Selling Your Horse

If you are truly committed to finding a good home for your horse, you need to ask potential buyers a lot of questions. For instance, ask the buyer for information about previous riding experience, and at least make sure that the buyer can saddle and bridle a horse before letting him ride. Also ask questions about the buyer's facilities—the ratio of stalls to horses, the kind of fence being used, the kind of hay and grain the horse will be fed and how much, and how many feedings per day.

It is also important for you to be honest about training and disposition issues. Just because the horse is a little angel when you are in the saddle, it doesn't necessarily mean the same horse will behave for a rank stranger. If Old Paint gets offended when some yahoo kicks him in the ribs, he may just decide that a few well-timed rodeo bucks will quickly unload the source of aggravation.

Some people just can't get along with some horses. Even if the horse is well behaved on the seller's property, he may not appreciate the change of address and may take his frustration out on the new owner.

Lease Agreements

The ideal situation might be to set up a lease agreement, with an option to buy. The buyer could try out the horse for a specified period of time, but the seller would retain ownership until both parties were satisfied that the relationship was going to work.

There are several advantages to lease agreements. Some potential horse buyers are smart enough to know that horse/human partnerships can get complicated. They are realistic about their own abilities and justifiably paranoid about ending up with more horse than they can handle. Most buyers would also like to make sure that the horse they are buying is appropriate for the riding activity they have in mind.

For instance, a trail rider, in the market for a bombproof peanut-pusher, might not appreciate the abilities of a champion barrel horse. Especially if the barrel horse is an excitable animal that bolts down the trail at the sight of a carnivorous bunny rabbit. The trail rider might well be impressed by the fact that his new horse can whiz around narrow turns at forty miles per hour, but he would probably prefer to travel at three miles per hour, a speed more conducive to enjoying the scenery.

Under a lease agreement, the horse may be able to stay at his original home. You would still be able to see the horse every day and make sure the animal is properly cared for. This arrangement also benefits buyers who don't own horse property. Many potential buyers would love to own a horse, but they can't fit one into a small apartment. If housing issues were taken care of, they would willingly share financial responsibility as well as barn chores.

If the horse is being kept at your home, the buyer may help pay maintenance costs. The buyer might also assume some barn chores, especially if you have health issues. If the horse is being kept at a boarding facility, you might exchange riding privileges for boarding fees. Veterinary bills would customarily still be your responsibility.

Under a lease agreement, you would be able to observe and influence interactions between the horse and buyer. The buyer would be able to ask your advice on any problems encountered while handling and riding the horse. In addition, the buyer would have an opportunity to get to know the horse, under your supervision, before the sale is final.

An amateur buyer would have the opportunity to learn about the responsibilities of horse ownership before committing himself to the final purchase. A great many people dream of horse ownership, but they do not realize how much work and expense is involved in keeping horses fed, groomed, housed, and trained.

A lawyer's advice should be sought before signing a lease agreement. Liability issues need to be explored, such as who would be responsible in the event of accident or injury. If the horse is injured, who will be responsible for vet bills? If a bystander is injured because the horse escaped from the buyer, or if the buyer is injured, who will be liable?

Other issues also need to be decided. Will the lease agreement be on a month-by-month basis, last for several months to a year, or able to be terminated any time, at your discretion? Also discuss whether the lease is renewable or not.

Determine housing arrangements—whether the horse will live at your residence, the buyer's residence, or at a boarding stable. Establish ahead of time who is responsible for bills, including farrier work, veterinary care, feed, housing, and even bedding supplies. Standards of care should be established, and you should be able to cancel the lease if the horse is being neglected or abused in any way.

A seller who takes the time to advertise, by putting up notices in local feed stores, tack shops, newspapers, and on the Internet, has a better chance of finding a good home for a horse. Many Internet sites offer free horse advertising, as well as a larger audience. Sites such as www.freehorseads.com offer basic text ads for free, but they charge for photo ads. Other sites, such as www.thehorseexchange.com, may offer free text and photo ads, but ask for a small voluntary donation once the horse is sold.

Finding Homes for Horses with Health and Safety Issues

Prospects of finding homes for horses with serious health and safety issues are dismal, although you might be lucky enough to find some kindhearted person to take one in for free as a pasture buddy for another horse. Finding a home for a young, green-broke horse with training issues is also a concern. If the young horse is well bred, a buyer will be more likely to invest the money needed to finish the animal's schooling. However, young grade horses, especially if they are not particularly attractive, have less chance of a bright future. Responsible owners may want to consider donating the horse to a rescue facility.

Finding Homes for Older Horses

Finding a good, long-term home for older horses is a concern. New owners may not want to risk dealing with added medical expenses that often go along with owning an older horse.

Gentle, well-trained older horses can be donated to therapeutic riding programs, as long as they are still sound enough for regular work. Organizations such as the North American Riding for the Handicapped Association (www.narha.org) have therapy centers in different parts of the country, and they can provide information on donating a horse.

Surrendering a Horse to a Rescue Facility

Horse rescue facilities may be the answer for owners committed to finding a secure home for grade horses with health or safety issues. Of course, an owner surrendering a horse to one of these facilities will not receive any monetary compensation for the animal. Some rescue facilities may charge a fee to help defray the costs of caring for a donated horse. The only compensation the owner will receive is the knowledge that the horse is being placed in a good home, and his welfare is being monitored.

Unfortunately, rescue facilities are often forced to put limitations on the type of horse they can accept. Horses with extremely violent behavioral problems may be unacceptable, due to the fact that the volunteers staffing such places may not include expert horse folk with training expertise. Horses with terminal illnesses, or illnesses that require prohibitively expensive long-term medical care, may also be unacceptable, as rescue facilities are often short of money.

A rescue may keep your horse at their facility or put him up for adoption. Potential adopters are screened by the facility. The process generally starts with an application. The application may require references who can vouch for the applicant's capabilities and include detailed instructions about feeding, housing, and veterinary and farrier care to be provided for the horse. The adopter may be asked to submit to inspections to make sure that the horse is being properly cared for. Applications commonly stipulate that the adopter must not sell the horse, and that the horse must be returned to the facility if the adopter is no longer able to care for him.

There is a list of rescue organizations in the appendix at the end of this book. It includes a wide variety of rescue organizations. Facilities that are not currently accepting donated horses will often provide other services, such as posting horses on a Web site or putting the owner in contact with potential adopters.

An owner should always check out the facilities personally before making the decision to surrender a horse to any rescue organization. There is no guarantee that the organizations will be able to give your horse a home. Such organizations are often short of money, space, and volunteers, and they may be unable to take your horse at the present time. Horse rescue facilities need and deserve all the monetary support they can get. They also need feed materials and equipment, as well as volunteers to help with horse care, fence building, and other chores.

If a facility cannot accept your horse due to lack of funds or overcrowding, they may still be able to help you find a home for your horse. Horse rescue organizations will often put your horse on their Web site so that potential adopters may contact you, or they may direct you to contact other organizations that might be able to help.

Appendix I

Dan Bowman: Natural Horsemanship Trainer and Clinician

Dan Bowman

Dan Bowman has worked with master horse trainers such as Ray Hunt, Buck Brannaman, and Craig Cameron. He has conducted riding clinics around the country, and he teaches natural horsemanship on his twenty-eight-acre ranch in Indiana, working with both horses and riders. Dan has also produced several videotapes to demonstrate his methods. *Western Horseman* magazine reviewed his training tapes and published the following comments in January 2002: "Dan Bowman uses a common-sense approach to explain how understanding the way horses think can help riders better communicate with and teach their horses."

Dan has been working with horses for forty years, and he started out using traditional methods. He began questioning these methods because a trainer to whom he was apprenticed nearly got him killed. While Dan was still recovering from that incident, he called up the late, great Tom Dorrance to ask for advice. Dorrance had started the whole resistance-free movement. He was a generous man, willing to share his vast knowledge of equine behavior. "That horse wasn't really trying to hurt you," he informed Dan. "He just wasn't ready to do what you were trying to accomplish with him."

Dan's conversations with Tom Dorrance were a life-changing experience that spurred an interest in resistance-free training methods. Over the following years, Dan worked with many well-known resistance-free trainers, but his favorite mentor was Craig Cameron. Craig's ability to communicate with aspiring horse trainers impressed Dan as much as the horse-training methods he demonstrated.

Dan believes that the ability to communicate with the human half of the horse/human partnership is vital to resistance-free training techniques. "It doesn't matter how well I have trained the horse if the owner still has the same bad habits," he says. "For the partnership to work, the owner has to be trained to get the correct response from the horse. It is critical for the owner to participate in the process of resistance-free training. If the owner hasn't changed when I send the horse back, then things will start to fall apart. The horse seeks the level of the rider. Some people believe that they don't need to know anything to have horses, but there is a world of difference between having horses and knowing horses."

Dan had accumulated twenty years of riding experience before he started investigating natural-horsemanship methods. Although all the years spent with horses were enjoyable, he wanted to know more. "Riding longer makes you a more experienced rider. It does not mean you will learn how to train a horse. Training knowledge must be acquired from a professional trainer who knows his business. All the great horse trainers had mentors who were kind enough to share their knowledge."

Although people may have owned horses for years, experience isn't everything. Knowledge is what enables horse people to be confident and safe while enjoying their pastime. You may have baby-soft hands, Velcro legs, and the balance of a PBR rodeo cowboy, but there is more to riding a horse than not falling off . You can't just ride your way through every horse problem.

For example, if a horse rears under saddle, an accomplished rider can throw his body weight forward, then urge the horse forward and into a turn. This action will bring the horse back down to earth, but it doesn't address the root cause of the behavior. The horse still hasn't learned anything and had probably misbehaved earlier. Rearing was simply the last thing he did. The root cause of the problem may be a serious gap in training.

Rearing can be a symptom of a problem with vertical flexion, causing the horse to rear up in a claustrophobic attempt to escape rein pressure. Training in vertical flexion teaches a horse to bend at the poll, tip his nose down, and give to rein pressure, as opposed to more unpleasant responses, such as rearing, bolting, or pushing and leaning on the bit. A horse's natural instinct is to push back and resist pressure. This is why softness, or lack of resistance, must be taught.

According to Dan, the definition of resistance-free or natural horsemanship is learning to "think like a horse." Part of learning to think like a horse, has to do with understanding the equine language. Horses may vocalize, but they communicate almost entirely by body language. Although we have the option of speaking, humans communicate by body language as much as 80 percent of the time. You and your horse are having a conversation every time you come in contact, whether you realize it or not. The horse can read human body language. He can tell if you are confident, intimidated, or angry. Often human body language communicates information we would rather the horse didn't know, revealing feelings of anger or aggression. Humans must learn how to use equine body language correctly in order to get the right message across.

The right message to convey to a horse is that the trainer is the alpha horse in the herd. The alpha horse in the herd controls the movements of the other horses, and provides leadership, food, safety, and security. A major goal of resistance-free training is to teach the horse to trust and respect the trainer's authority in tense situations, instead of shying or running away.

One method used to put the trainer in the alpha-horse position is round-pen training. Round-pen work confines the horse in a small enough area to keep his attention on the trainer, without inducing a claustrophobic reaction. The horse is confined, but he still has a choice whether to come to the trainer or not. For that reason, the round pen should be a least 50 to 60 feet in diameter, so that too much pressure is not put on the animal.

To quote Dan, "the goal of round-pen training is not to run a horse around in a circle until the animal gets tired. The goal is to make the horse want to come to the trainer as a source of comfort and leadership, to accept the trainer as the alpha horse in the partnership." This process is known as "join-up" or "hooking on." The join-up process also teaches the horse to seek out the trainer as a source of comfort and security. Round-pen training helps prepare the horse emotionally for training. If done right, round-pen training makes the horse want to be with the trainer, as well as establishing the idea that the trainer can control the horse's movements without causing pain. Round-pen training helps establish a relationship with the horse that is based on trust, not fear or violence.

Work in the round pen makes the right choices (trust and respect) easy and the wrong choice (resistance) hard. The trainer directs the movements of the horse by using body language. A lasso may also be used to help drive the horse's movements. This process of directing and driving introduces a basic principle of impulsion used throughout the process of resistance-free training.

Once the horse "joins up," the trainer rubs and handles every part of the horse. He may pick up the horse's feet and rub a rope or blanket all over the animal to sack him out. Some trainers even saddle and ride a horse during this first session in the round pen, but Dan prefers not to risk overwhelming the horse with too much information at once.

Other techniques employed in resistance-free training involve continued groundwork. This groundwork involves teaching the horse to yield to pressure and to look for the release from that pressure. It is much safer to teach such skills as breaking at the poll, backing up, and disengaging the hindquarters from the ground. A horse that hasn't been taught to give to pressure and how to correctly, calmly, and consistently seek release from pressure during groundwork, may decide to rear in an attempt to escape that pressure with a rider in the saddle. A horse that hasn't been taught to seek release from pressure by stopping may bolt. A horse that hasn't been taught how to seek release from pressure may pull back on a lead rope when led or tied.

"Pressure and release" is one of the most important principle of resistance-free training, and it is one of the hardest to learn, because it requires patience. Most people simply do not have the patience to "wait on the horse." An example of this is teaching a horse to back up. Sometimes, even a horse that willingly backs during groundwork will refuse to back with a rider in the saddle.

Dan demonstrates the correct way to teach a horse to back up in one of his "Classroom in the Corral" tapes, titled *Speaking from the Saddle*. Using gentle pressure on one rein, he waits for the front foot on that side to move back one step, then immediately releases the pressure. Even if the horse only takes the weight off the desired foot, Dan immediately releases pressure. Dan believes that it is important to wait for the horse to solve the problem by figuring out that he gets a release from pressure by backing up.

Though you may be able to *force* a horse to physically do something with pain and pressure, the only way you *teach* him anything is by teaching him to seek release from pressure. Dan says that release from pressure is the "yes" answer that tells the horse that he has done the right thing.

Pressure and release is a form of sensitization training. You want your horse to become more sensitive to pressure. If you keep pulling on a horse's mouth, you desensitize him to bit pressure. In the old days, Western riding instructors would often tell students to "stay out of a horse's mouth." The idea is to cease pressure on the reins as soon as the horse does what you want or even tries to do what you want.

"Advance and Retreat," another important principle of natural horsemanship, is a form of desensitization training. An example of the advance-and-retreat method is teaching a young horse to accept having his legs and feet handled. Advance and retreat involves de-sensitizing the horse to an action by slowly and patiently working up to the eventual goal by "baby steps." Each step is repeated until the horse relaxes and calmly accepts each step in the process.

Instead of directly reaching for a hoof, you might start by repeat-edly stroking the tops of the horse's legs, backing off each time the horse relaxes, then slowly moving further down the leg, until you can touch and stroke the entire leg. Eventually you move on to picking up the horse's foot momentarily, then gently placing it back on the ground, until the horse is comfortable with having his feet picked up.

It is important to back off when the horse relaxes and gives the correct response. Backing off is the reward for the correct response, as well as reassurance. You are telling the horse, "that's all I wanted."

Retreating and allowing the horse to relax before you proceed with desensitization also reassures a fearful horse that you are not a predator. Predators tend to go after what they want in a straight line and attack vulnerable body parts, such as the legs. Fearful horses re-spond best to advance-and-retreat methods. Disrespectful horses may require firmer methods. All horses should be taught to yield their hindquarters and to stand still before such training begins.

Relying on pain and physical force to train a horse may have unpleasant consequences, such as bucking, bolting, and rearing. Resistance-free trainers, such as Dan Bowman, believe there is a better way. Dan believes a horse needs to be trained physically, mentally, and emotionally. In his opinion, having the horse emotionally ready to perform a task is every bit as important as the first two, but it is too often neglected.

According to Dan, you can *physically* turn a horse by pulling on one rein hard enough to force him to the right or left, but the horse will be tensed up and resistant to pressure. Or you can have him *mentally* ready to turn by teaching him to respond to the slightest rein pressure. Still, the horse may be tensed up and not giving the best performance. Only after a foundation of trust and respect has been established will a horse perform calmly, consistently, and willingly. Only then is the horse *emotionally* ready to perform. The goal of natural horsemanship and resistance-free training is a finished horse that is physically, mentally, and emotionally ready to perform.

Though resistance-free methods are useful in dealing with problem horses, Dan urges caution when dealing with abused horses. "We need to use common sense about what we are doing. Don't put yourself in a position where you or the horse can get hurt. Understand the limits of your own ability. Don't let your ego get you in trouble."

"We all like to think positive, we all like to think that we can do more than we can," Dan says. "Be realistic regarding your abilities. Understand that you are not a professional trainer. Understand going in that if you adopt an abused horse, you may have to spend a lot of money to hire a professional trainer, and there is still no guarantee that you will be able to handle the horse when you get it back home. Your knowledge must be equal to the task, or you could wind up in the hospital."

Tapes Featuring Dan Bowman's Natural Horsemanship Program

Vol #1: Round Pen Junction: This tape covers the basics of round-pen training theory, with emphasis on safety for horse and handler. Dan prepares the horse mentally for training, explains how to use body language to communicate with a horse, and demonstrates how to use a round pen to establish a relationship with the horse that incorporates both trust and leadership. He explains basic natural-horsemanship concepts such as direct and drive, advance and retreat, pressure and release.

Vol #2: Hors'n Around on the Ground: The second tape features exercises to physically prepare a horse for training by using more advanced groundwork. Dan prepares a young horse for riding by sacking him out, and he explains related concepts such as "changing eyes," which are important in preparing a young horse for riding. Using a twelve-foot lead rope, Dan shows how to train for vertical flexibility, pressure and release, yielding the hindquarters, and performing a one-rein stop during groundwork.

Vol #3: Speaking from the Saddle: A very user-friendly tape that covers a lot of ground, from tacking up a horse safely to teaching the side-pass. The segment on teaching a horse to back up using pressure-and-release techniques is especially good. Some of the other topics covered include teaching a horse to neck rein, one-rein stop, and how to negotiate hills on the trail. There is an important segment on performing a one-rein stop as a necessary tool for riding safely.

Vol #4: Unplug Your Horse: A very interesting tape, covering some areas you don't see in most horse-training videos. A young horse is trained to accept being hobbled as a means of teaching patience and helping him learn to stand still. A horse with a previous history of rearing up and falling over backwards is introduced to ground-driving and is also bitted up. These methods are employed to teach him vertical and lateral flexion, which will help to correct his dangerous behavior without endangering a rider.

Vol #5: Baby's First Ride and More: Though a lot of ground is covered on this DVD, Dan is a great communicator, his instructions are clear and easy to understand, and the video segments illustrating his techniques are well done. The first part of the DVD covers the groundwork necessary to prepare a colt for riding. Getting the colt's attention, speed and direction control, and pressure-and-release concepts are demonstrated. An exercise focused on teaching a colt to "change eyes" is included.

Dan then proceeds to the first saddling and employs ground-driving techniques to teach the colt to respond to the reins before ever climbing into the saddle. During the first ride, Dan demonstrates how to control the colt and keep him calm. He teaches the colt to change directions, change speeds, back up, move his forehand and hindquarters over, and back up without the aid of a bit. Dan also demonstrates the safest and best way to execute a one-rein stop, which is critical before a young horse can be ridden out of a confined area.

You can order tapes or contact Dan Bowman at the following address:

Dan Bowman
Lazy B Ranch
28832 Blue Creek Road
Sunman, Indiana 47041
Phone: (812) 623–3761
www.danbowman.net

Appendix II

List of Horse Rescue Organizations and Adoption Facilities

The following list of equine rescue organizations and adoption facilities should be checked out personally by anyone who wishes to donate to or adopt a horse from any of these facilities. Try to choose an organization that has been in existence for a number of years. Organizations should also be accredited by well-regarded animal welfare groups, such as the ASPCA, Hooved Animal Humane Society, government agencies such as the Bureau of Land Management, or a recognized breed organization such as the USTA Standardbred Equine Program. Organizations with 501(c)(3) charitable organization status are also more likely to be legitimate. A rescue agency's charitable status can be checked using Guide Star (www.guidestar.org) or the IRS Search for Charities (www.irs.gov/charities/article/O,,id=96136.oo.html).

Thoroughbreds

ReRun, Inc.

ReRun specializes in finding good homes for nonracing thoroughbreds and has chapters in New York, Virginia, New Jersey, and

Kentucky. ReRun will accept ex-racehorses for adoption, providing they have room and the horse does not have a medical condition that would cause an undue hardship on the organization. ReRun charges the owner a small initial donation fee to help pay for the expenses of caring for the horse. If the organization is unable to find room for the horse, they will try to help the owner locate another retirement facility. When owners donate their retired thoroughbreds to ReRun, the organization prepares each horse for a lifetime home with capable, responsible adopters.

Adopting Horses from ReRun, Inc.

Potential adopters start the process by filling out an application form. They must also supply references and pay a minimal adoption fee. Prior to adoption, a potential adopter may request a veterinary exam at his or her own expense. After all requirements are met, the adopter signs a Lifetime Care Agreement.

When adopting an ex-racehorse, some retraining is usually necessary. ReRun has on-site trainers to reschool ex-racehorses and prepare them for adoption. The organization makes its best effort to offer sane, sound horses to potential adopters. They also try to match each horse to the skill level of the adopter.

> **Re-Run, Inc.**
> **c/o Laurie Lane**
> **P.O. Box 113**
> **Helmetta, NJ 08828**
> **Web site: www.rerun.org**

Additional Thoroughbred Resources

Thoroughbred Retirement Foundation

PMB 351, 450 Shrewsbury Plaza
Shrewsbury, NJ 07702–4332
Phone: (732) 957–0182
Web site: www.trfinc.org/

Canter USA
Web site: www.canterusa.org

Standardbreds

The American Standardbred Adoption Program

The American Standardbred Adoption Program, a 501(c)(3) charitable organization, accepts donated nonracing standardbreds and adopts them out. The ASAP also provides sanctuary for abused and neglected horses of other breeds, and it is listed with the Humane Society of the United States.

ASAP Adoption Procedure

Like most organizations of its kind, the goal of the ASAP is to find stable, lifetime homes with responsible caregivers for the horses in its care. With this goal in mind, the ASAP requires that potential adopters pass a screening process. Step one of this process includes filling out an application. Aside from basic data, such as the name and address of the adopter, the first two sections of the application ask for the adopter's preferences for the age, size, and sex of the horse to be adopted.

The ASAP will want to know information regarding the adopter's experience with horses, as well as the activities in which the horse will be expected to engage, such as trail riding, showing, or therapy work with handicapped individuals. The applicant will need to provide veterinary and farrier references. Adequate farrier and veterinary care, including regular inoculations, are a condition of adoption.

ASAP Donation Procedure

Donating a standardbred horse to the ASAP benefits both the horse and owner. An owner donating an ex-racehorse to the ASAP may be eligible for a tax deduction representing part of the value of the horse. The owner also has the comfort of knowing that ASAP personnel will do their level best to ensure that the horse will have a loving, stable home for life.

ASAP Farm and Office
S6039A Pedretti Lane
De Soto, WI 54624
Phone: (608) 689–2399
Web site: www.4thehorses.com
E-mail: asapinc@mwt.net

PMU Foals

Equine Angels Rescue Sanctuary

Equine Angels Rescue Sanctuary has grade and registered PMU foals available for adoption. Registered foals available include quarter horses and paints. Draft crosses are also available. Certain requirements must be met before adopting foals from the EARS facility. Though a potential adopter's farm may be set up well for full-grown horses, foals have special needs. Fencing has to be foal-safe. EARS personnel recommend diamond-weave fencing with openings too small for little hooves to go through. Modular panels or round-pen panels will also work.

Those wishing to adopt a foal from EARS will need to sign an adoption agreement and fill out an adoption application. The adoption agreement requires the adopter to provide basic care for the foal, such as adequate shelter, a safe and secure pasture, veterinary care including yearly inoculations, and farrier care. Breeding of horses is prohibited, and stallions must be gelded.

The adoption application requires adopters to provide information on previous experience with horses, provide farrier and veterinary references, and submit to site inspections. Adoption fees vary, depending on breed, color, and amount of training the horse has received. EARS can deliver horses to the adopter's residence, although there is a charge for this service.

EARS
214 Candlewood Mountain Road
New Milford, CT 06776
Phone: (203) 733–3576
Web site: www.foalrescue.com

Mustangs

Prison Programs

The Wyoming Honor Farm has saddle-trained horses available for adoption, and wild horse training clinics at some of their scheduled events. Internet adoptions are also available.

Wyoming Honor Farm
40 Honor Farm Road
Riverton, Wyoming 82501
Phone: (307) 856–9878
Web site: http://doc.state.wy.us/prisons/horse_adoption.asp

The James Crabtree Correctional Center in Helena, Oklahoma, is a year-round mustang-holding facility, and potential adopters may make an appointment to adopt a mustang at any time of year, subject to approval by the BLM. On-site training services are also available to mustang adopters.

Oklahoma Department of Corrections
James Crabtree Correctional Center
Helena, OK 73741
Phone: (580) 852–3221

The Nevada Department of Corrections Warm Springs Correctional Center
Carson City, NV 89701
Phone: (775) 861–6469
Web site: www.nv.blm.gov/prison_horses/

Inmate Management Hutchinson Correctional Facility
Hutchinson/Valley Center
Hutchinson, Kansas
Phone: (620) 728–3296
Web site: www.dc.state.ks.us/hcf/standard/default.html

Additional Government Resources for Wild Burros and Mustangs

A list of mustang and wild burro adoption sites, addresses, phone numbers, and schedules can be obtained at www.wildhorseandburro .blm.gov/schedule.

Mustang adoption sites are located all over the country, from Ventura, California to Okeechobee, Florida. Information can also be obtained by writing or calling the BLM state office for your area. A listing of state offices is available on the web at www.igha.org/ BLM5.html.

Mustangs can also be adopted over the Internet. Information is located at the Bureau of Land Management Wild Horse and Burro Internet Adoption site at www.blm.gov/adoptahorse/.

Rescue Organizations by State

Alabama

Decatur, Alabama BLM Mustang Adoption Site
Jackson Field Office
Phone: (888) 274–2133

Alaska

Alaska Equine Rescue
P. O. Box 113265
Anchorage, Alaska 99511–3265
Phone: (888) 588–4677
E-mail: aer@alaskaequinerescue.com

Arizona

The Horse Rescue of North Scottsdale
6631 E. Montgomery Rd.
Cave Creek, AZ 85254
Phone: (602) 689–8825

Kingman Regional Wild Horse and Burro Facility
BLM facility. Wild horse and burro adoptions held monthly.
Phone: (928) 692–400

Arkansas

Humane Society of Marion County
P.O. Box 1384
Yellville, Arkansas 72687
Phone: (870) 449–8668

California

Equus Sanctuary
P.O. Box 9
Ravensdale, CA 96132
Phone: (530) 931–0108

Litchfield Wild Horse and Burro Corrals
BLM facility. Wild horse and burro adoptions only.
Phone: (530) 254–6575

The Phoenix Equine Foundation
P.O. Box 1235
Glen Ellen, CA 95442
Web site: www.extendinc.com/phoenix

True Innocents Equine Rescue (T.I.E.R.)
7900 Limonite Ave., Ste. G, #278
Riverside, CA 92509
Phone: (951) 360–1464
E-mail: info@TIERRescue.org

Colorado

Colorado Department of Corrections Canon City Facility
Gentled mustangs available for adoption through the Colorado Department of Corrections.
Wild Horse Inmate Program
P.O. Box 1600, Canon Complex
Canon City, CO 81215-1600
Telephone: (719) 269–8539

Colorado Horse Rescue
10386 North 65th Street
Longmont, CO 80503
Phone: (720) 494–1414

Connecticut

Equine Angels Rescue Sanctuary
214 Candlewood Mountain Road
New Milford, CT 06776
Phone: (203) 733–3576
Web site: www.foalrescue.com

Delaware

Tri-State Equine Adoption and Rescue
869 Hartly Road
Hartly, DE 19953
Web site: www.tristateequine.org

Florida

The Azizi Foundation
Leighton Farms Ave.
Palm City, FL 34990
Phone: (772) 334–6681
E-mail: azizi@aol.com

LB Ranch
Myakka City, FL 34251
Phone: (941) 322–1630

Georgia

Georgia Equine Rescue League
P.O. Box 787
Locust Grove, Georgia 30248
Phone: (770) 464–0138
Web site: www.gerlltd.org

Illinois

Crosswinds Equine Rescue, Inc.
1476 N. County Route 1350E
Tuscola, IL 61953
Phone: (217) 832–2010
Web site: www.crosswindseqresq.org
E-mail: info@cwer.org

Eastern States Wild Horse and Burro Facility at Ewing
Wild horse and burro adoptions.
Phone: (800) 370–3936

Hooved Animal Humane Society
10804 McConnell Road
Woodstock, IL 60098
Phone: (815) 337–5563

Indiana

Indiana Horse Rescue
916 South Prairie Avenue
Frankfort, IN 46041
Phone: (765) 659–5209

Kentucky

Equine Transitional Training Alliance, Inc.
P.O. Box 24834
Lexington, KY 40524
Phone: (859) 846–5655

Thoroughbred Retirement Foundation
TRF accepts surrendered thoroughbred racehorses. Acceptance is subject to restrictions. Thoroughbred sport horses are only accepted if they can go directly to an adoptive home. Owners are expected to contribute to the support of the surrendered horse if they are financially able.
Secretariat Center
4089 Ironworks Parkway
Lexington, KY 40511
Phone: (859) 246–3080

Louisiana

Hopeful Haven Equine Rescue
P.O. Box 17783
Shreveport, LA 71138
Phone: (318) 390–9161
E-mail: hopefulhaven@yahoo.com

Maine

Adopt A Horse
Pamela Morse
P.O. Box 1
Fairfield, ME 04937
Phone: (207) 453–0052
E-mail: pamel@mint.net

Maryland

Day's End Farm Horse Rescue
15856 Frederick Road
Lisbon, MD 21765

Massachusetts

MSPCA at Nevins Farm
400 Broadway
Methuen, MA 01844
Phone: (978) 687–7453

Michigan

Canter
2760 East Lansing Drive, Suite 5
East Lansing, MI 48823
E-mail: cantermichigan@canterusa.org

Missouri

D-D Farm, Animal Sanctuary and Rescue
C. Dale and Debbie Tolentino
6000 North Creasy Springs Road
Columbia, MO 65202
E-mail: ddfarm@tranquility.net

Humane Society of Missouri Longmeadow Rescue Ranch
Union, Missouri
Phone: (636) 583–8759
Web site: www.longmeadowrescueranch.org

Montana

Montana Large Animal Sanctuary and Rescue
P. O. Box 99
Hot Springs, MT 59845
Phone: (406) 741–3823
E-mail: info@mtanimalsanctuary.com

Nebraska

Elm Creek Wild Horse and Burro Center
BLM primary preparation center for wild horses and burros gathered from public lands in Nevada. Site schedules regular adoption events and also schedules individual adoptions.
Phone: (308) 856–4498

Nevada

National Wild Horse and Burro Center at Palomino Valley
BLM primary preparation center for wild horses and burros gathered from public lands in Nevada.
Phone: (775) 475–2222
Nevada Department of Corrections
Phone: (775) 861–6469
Web site: www.nv.gov/prison_horses

New Hampshire

Live and Let Live Farm
20 Paradise Lane
Chichester, NH 03258
Phone: (603) 798–5615
Web site: www.liveandletlivefarm.org

North Carolina

United States Equine Rescue League

USERL is not currently accepting surrendered horses, except from animal control. However, they provide a page on their Web site to help link owners who can no longer care for their horses with potential adopters.

P.O. Box 914
Culpepper, VA 22701
Phone: (336) 720–9257 in North Carolina
(703) 580–9199 in Virginia
Web site: www.ncerl.com

Ohio

Humane Society of Delaware County
c/o Horse Rescue Fund
4920 State Route 37 East
Delaware, OH 43015
Phone: (740) 369–7387

Voices for Horses Rescue Network
P.O. Box 566
Toledo, OH 43697-0566
Phone: (419) 247–0025
E-mail: voiceforhorses@wmconnect.com

Oklahoma

Pauls Valley Adoption Center
BLM resting area for wild horses and burros arriving from the West. Animals are available for adoption the second Tuesday of the month.
Phone: (800) 237–3642

Oregon

Burns District Wild Horse Corrals
Primary BLM preparation area for wild horses gathered in Oregon. Home of the famous Kiger Herd.
Phone: (541) 573–4456 or (541) 573–4439

Pennsylvania

Hog Heaven
2681 Mallory Road
Cochranton, PA 16314
Phone: (814) 425–1850

Lost & Found Horse Rescue Foundation, Inc.
852 Valley Road,
Jacobus, PA 17403
Phone: (717) 428–9701

Tennessee

Angel Rescue
3976 Highway 70 West
Dickson, Tennessee 37055
Phone: (615) 740–0964
Web site: www.angelrescue.com

Horse Haven of Tennessee, Inc.
P.O. Box 20392
Knoxville, TN 37940
Phone: (865) 609–4030

Texas

Lone Star Equine Rescue
P.O. Box 627
Haslet, TX 76052
Web site: www.lser.org

Utah

Delta Wild Horse and Burro Facility
BLM wild horse and burro holding facility. Adoptions by appointment only.
Phone: (307) 352–0292

Salt Lake Regional Wild Horse and Burro Center
BLM preparation center for horses gathered in Utah. Adoption by appointment.
Phone: (877) 224–3956

Virginia

The Laughing Horse Sanctuary
8317 Grassland Drive
Sandy Level, VA 24161
Phone: (434) 927–5297 or (434) 927–5298

Lost Fantasy Stables
P.O. Box 42
Ceres, VA 24318
Phone: (276) 682–3729

United States Equine Rescue League
USERL is not currently accepting surrendered horses, except from animal control. However, they provide a page on their Web site to help link owners who can no longer care for their horses with potential adopters.
P.O. Box 914
Culpepper, VA 22701
Phone: (336) 720–9257 in North Carolina
(703) 580–9199 in Virginia
Web site: www.ncerl.com

Washington

Pacific Equestrian Center Rescue Program
13615 SE 288th Street
Kent, WA 98042
Phone: (206) 551–5369
Web site: www.pacificequestriancenter.com

Second Chance Ranch
P.O. Box 899
Elma, WA 98541
Phone: (360) 861–8056
Web site: http://secondchanceranch.org

Wisconsin

Midwest Horse Welfare Foundation, Inc.
1055 Day Road
Marshfield, WI 54449
Phone: (715) 387–0555
Web site: www.equineadoption.com

Wyoming

Rock Springs Corrals
BLM wild horse preparation center.
Phone: (307) 352–0292

National Agencies

ASPCA
424 East 92nd St.
New York, NY 10128-6801
Phone: (212) 876–7700
Web site: www.aspca.org

The Humane Society of the United States
2100 L. Street NW
Washington DC 20037
Phone: (202) 452–1100
Web site: www.hsus.org